THE ENGINE
OF AMERICA

THE ENGINE OF AMERICA

THE SECRETS TO SMALL BUSINESS SUCCESS FROM ENTREPRENEURS WHO HAVE MADE IT!

HECTOR V. BARRETO

Former Administrator of the
U.S. Small Business Administration

with

ROBERT J. WAGMAN

John Wiley & Sons, Inc.

Published by John Wiley & Sons, Inc., Hoboken, New Jersey.
Published simultaneously in Canada.

Wiley Bicentennial Logo: Richard J. Pacifico

For general information on our other products and services or for technical support, please contact our Customer Care Department within the United States at (800) 762-2974, outside the United States at (317) 572-3993 or fax (317) 572-4002.

Wiley also publishes its books in a variety of electronic formats. Some content that appears in print may not be available in electronic books. For more information about Wiley products, visit our web site at www.wiley.com.

Library of Congress Cataloging-in-Publication Data:
Barreto, Hector V., 1961-
  The engine of America : the secrets to small business success from entrepreneurs who have made it! / Hector V. Barreto.
     p.   cm.
  ISBN 978-0-470-11013-3 (cloth)
  1. Small business—United States—Management. 2. Small business—United States—Finance. 3. New business enterprises—United States. 4. Entrepreneurship—United States. 5. Success in business—United States.   I. Title. II. Title: Keys to small business success from entrepreneurs.
  HD62.7.B366 2007
  658.02'2—dc22   2007018925

Printed in the United States of America

10   9   8   7   6   5   4   3   2   1

*To the first entrepreneurs I ever met—Mary Louise and Hector Barreto Sr.,
my parents.*

*And to the most important people in my life: Robin, my wife; and my children
Avrial, Tahlia, and Julian—all three future entrepreneurs.*

Contents

Foreword

I have been privileged to work with leaders in science and medicine and the business arena for many years. During my tenure as chairman of the Nobel Family Society, I traveled to most parts of the world and still remain fascinated with the balance between common ideas that cross national borders and those specific traits that identify the soul of a nation.

To that end, there are few things more American than entrepreneurship. The bold spirit of risk taking—of starting with next to nothing and building more with dreams than with money—is vintage American. Now, that is not to say that most of the Western world and more recently the other part of the globe from Russia to China have not accepted the concept of small business—of start-ups and developing enterprises and mergers.

However, if the history books could track it and the statisticians could measure it, that special spirit that saturates the world of small business would most likely find its roots somewhere in Kansas or Vermont or Georgia or Arizona. They would also find that the

United States happily accepts the eruption of entrepreneurship, which has resulted in most new jobs today being created by small firms. Of the exporters in business today, 97 percent are small businesses.

In fact, the president of the United States has described the exponential growth of small business as establishing a new engine to drive the American economy. In practically every industry, the largest companies are being shadowed by the growth and imagination of thousands of small firms.

The former leader of the U.S. Small Business Administration has now created an excellent tool for them. It is easy to use, it is certainly affordable, and it certainly works. The next generation of small business owners and the generations who follow will thank Hector Barreto for this tool.

My friend Hector Barreto's new book, *The Engine of America,* provides some very lucid, incisive, and pertinent explanations of how dozens of small firms can grow into big-time business, often within a short time. The book tracks the leap of faith from starting point to start up and then up the ladder. Hector has brought to the table, in this case to the book, willing role models who are not afraid to admit that something other than their own wit and work helped bring about their own success.

We discover the guidelines, the timing, and the challenges to be avoided when starting or growing a business in almost every imaginable field. CEOs and other senior executives candidly provide the reader with remarkable insights. The rest is up to him or her.

Hector Barreto likes to say that small business wants the same thing as big business—more business. This book offers a road map and a blueprint to help that happen.

You should read this book if you are serious about learning from those who shared a dream of success and created their own reality. As for Hector Barreto, after administering the multibillion-dollar loan efforts of a nation to assist small business growth, he now offers a different but equally impressive contribution. Here is the knowledge, the experience, and the passion of those who have made it and met its multitude of challenges. Read it, this book will help you to join that list.

Professor Michael Nobel, PhD
Stockholm, Sweden

Acknowledgments

I want to thank the remarkable team of dedicated career employees and administration appointees at the Small Business Administration that I was privileged to serve with during my five-year tenure. The U.S. small business sector owes a debt of gratitude to great resource partners, like SCORE counselors, the Small Business Development Center professionals, the passionate Women Business Center advocates, and all of the individuals who dedicate themselves to training and counseling small business persons.

This book would not have come about without my friend and colleague Chuck Ashman's insistence that that it needed to be written, and the invaluable research and editorial contributions of my friend, colleague, and collaborator Bob Wagman. I want to thank Carol Ann Wagman for her editing skills.

I could never have completed this book without my patient wife Robin and our children, who gave me time and space while moving from Washington DC to California, changing careers, and writing this book.

I must also acknowledge my hard-working and loyal executive assistant Laura Person for her continued commitment and invaluable aid, all given with patience and good humor.

Kudos to the entire team at John Wiley & Sons, especially to Executive Vice President Steve Kippur, my diligent editor Matt Holt, and Jessica Campilango, Senior Production Editor Deborah Schindlar, and the production team at Publications Development Company, and to marketer Kim Dayman, publicist Jocelyn Cordova, Bonnie Redding, and PJ Campbell for their total support from the very beginning throughout this exciting project.

I am grateful to all of the entrepreneurs across the country and around the world that I have been able to work with and learn from. They have been my mentors. I owe a debt of gratitude to all of the government officials and private sector executives who have partnered with me to empower small businesses including leaders throughout the world, especially in Mexico and Latin America.

Special acknowledgment goes to the investment and true partnership that countless U.S. corporations have provided to support and empower small business. Often, they do it as a guiding corporate imperative. There are too many to include all of them here, but special mention goes to Hewlitt Packard, American Airlines, Verizon, Wellpoint, Western Union, and AFLAC.

I must also thank the CEOs and other leaders of successful corporations who shared their ideas with me so as to provide opportunities for you. I am especially grateful to all of the special men and women who allowed me to interview them for this book and who made significant contributions to the end product. They are not only role models, but true champions—to name just a few: Alex Pitt, Bob Lorsch. John Soltesz, Rudy Estrada, Bob Lotter, Dick Raskin, Pepe Carral, Marty Winnick, Alex Meruelo, Mike Rezinas, Castulo de la Rocha, and David Lizzarraga—all have shown by example what entrepreneurship can accomplish. Thank you for sharing your wonderful experiences.

From the beginning, I have been blessed to work with fine colleagues and businesses. My first coworkers were my wonderful sisters, Anna Favrow, Gloria Smith, Rosa Dobson, and Mary Shearhart.

Finally, thanks to my late beloved father who inspired me and was my hero and my wonderful mother who taught me to be independent, resourceful, and gave me everything I "really" needed to achieve my dreams.

THE ENGINE
OF AMERICA

I

The Journey Begins

1

My Life in and around Small Businesses

There is much in this book to help the small business owner or, more important, the person who is thinking about starting a business. It helps small business owners who are just getting started or owners of established businesses that are now in the process of growing into moderate-size enterprises on the way to becoming big businesses. Many of today's dominant and successful corporations started as small businesses—some in garages, basements, or home offices.

I have been involved in small businesses all my life: first in my parents' businesses, then my own, and for five years I was the administrator of the U.S. Small Business Administration (SBA), the federal government's agency with the responsibility to advise, counsel, assist, and protect America's small businesses. I have seen small businesses that are thriving and I have, regretfully and sometimes even tragically, seen small businesses that fail despite being based on sound ideas that had the most dedicated of owners.

I understand what makes some small businesses succeed while others similarly situated fail. This book shares the insights I have gained about small business success and small business failure.

During my tenure as head of the SBA, I faced a bleak statistic: Every year millions of new small businesses are started. Although each owner is passionate and driven, and believes deeply that his or her new business will succeed, a majority of these new small businesses will fail. It's the old story—they never plan to fail, but often do because they fail to plan.

In 2001, when I became the SBA administrator, the SBA's independent research arm, the Office of Advocacy, forecast that within five years fully 50 percent of newly started small businesses would fail—be unable to continue operation. Unfortunately, over the five-plus years I was at the SBA, we were not able to do anything to lower this percentage; in fact, things have gotten worse. Currently, the Office of Advocacy reports:

> Two-thirds of new employer establishments survive at least two years, and 44 percent survive at least four years, according to a recent study. These results were similar for different industries. Firms that began in the second quarter of 1998 were tracked for the next 16 quarters to determine their survival rate. Despite conventional wisdom that restaurants fail much more frequently than firms in other industries, leisure and hospitality establishments, which include restaurants, survived at rates only slightly below the average. Earlier research has explored the reasons for a new business's survivability. Major factors in a firm's remaining open include an ample supply of capital, being large enough to have employees, the owner's education level, and the owner's reason for starting the firm in the first place, such as freedom for family life or wanting to be one's own boss.

But an important and critical distinction needs to be made: A business that ceases operation does not necessarily fail. Small Business Administration economist Brian Headd closely examined the survey data collected by the U.S. Census Bureau's Business Information Tracking Series and came to the following conclusion:

> New firms are believed to have high closure rates and these closures are believed to be failures, but two U.S. Census Bureau data sources illustrate that these assumptions may not be justified. . . . The significant proportion of businesses that closed while successful calls into question the use of

"business closure" as a meaningful measure of business outcome. It appears that many owners may have executed a planned exit strategy, closed a business without excess debt, sold a viable business, or retired from the workforce.

Headd also found:

Similar to previous studies, firms having more resources—that were larger, with better financing and having employees—were found to have better chances of survival. Factors that were characteristic of closure—such as having no start-up capital and having a relatively young owner—were also common in businesses considered successful at closure.

Let me repeat for emphasis: Just because a business closes, it hasn't necessarily failed. But many do fail; many more than should fail.

There are 25 million small businesses in the United States and they produce 52 percent of the gross domestic product of the U.S. economy. Small businesses represent over 50 percent of the employee payrolls in the economy, and somewhere between 60 percent and 70 percent of the new jobs our economy produces annually. We are simply losing too many of the newly started small businesses each year. It is damaging to the economy and its long-term growth.

No small business starts out planning to fail. Almost all are started by men or women who are passionate about what they are doing. They have a dream and are willing to work and sacrifice to attain that dream.

Why do these small businesses fail? As we see shortly, it is often that small business owners, especially those starting a business for the first time, simply do not know what they do not know. Perhaps in starting a new business, budding entrepreneurs are particularly excited about one aspect of the new business and they simply don't realize—or think about—all those other things they are going to have to do or the challenges they are going to have to meet. Worse, they usually don't learn these things until after they start a business and it starts struggling with these problems and challenges. The start-up owner doesn't plan to fail, but he or she fails because of the failure to plan.

Small businesses fail for a myriad of reasons: They were not good ideas in the first place; they were undercapitalized; the new owner did not have the ability to turn an idea into a business; or the owner in the end did not have the commitment it takes.

When a small business fails, you hear all kinds of explanations. One reason might have been a lack of capital. Capital is the oxygen that a small business needs to breathe—to get the business started and to grow the business. If the business lacks capital, it will struggle.

Often, a new business owner's expectations are simply not aligned with reality. When I first started in business, someone said to me, "Give yourself enough time to become profitable." So I thought to myself, "Okay, I'll give myself six months, a year at the most." Although that's what I planned for, it ended up taking me three to four years to build the business, develop the client base, and become profitable. Because I was starting from scratch, I did what many small businesses do: I couldn't qualify for a loan, so I used all my savings, maxed out my credit cards, cashed out my retirement from the corporate job I had held, borrowed some money when I could, and basically just limped along until my business was able to generate enough cash.

Underestimating how long it will be until the business becomes profitable is a major problem in starting up new businesses. Sometimes people glamorize the idea of being in business for themselves, but most people should not work for themselves. Not everyone has the discipline, energy, or long-term commitment it takes.

Again, it's not a failure to delay starting a business because you're not ready. Often the opposite—being unprepared—leads to failure. At the SBA, we thought it was a good thing to prevent an entrepreneur from making that mistake. If he or she was serious about starting a business, we would say, "It's not a question of *if*, it's a question of *when*. If you invest the time to be ready, and are prepared to sacrifice, we'll be there to stand shoulder to shoulder with you as your partner."

At the SBA, we learned three other reasons new businesses fail. First, they don't hire the right employees. A new business will take whoever they can—usually a family member or friend who is willing to work for little or nothing. They may not be the best employee for a new business, but the one they can afford.

Second, when a new business owner does not know how to use technology and if he or she is competing with established businesses, especially larger ones, it's going to be an issue. Technology really levels the playing field.

Third, we found that the novice business owner is sometimes unaware of the regulations or potential restrictions he or she will face and struggles to meet these requirements.

At the SBA, we tried to arm small business owners with the tools to address these problem areas, providing various programs that addressed: (1) access to capital, (2) technical assistance/entrepreneurial development, and (3) procurement/contracting. Small businesses are usually challenged in all of these areas: They don't have enough money; they don't have enough customers; and they don't know what they don't know.

These deficiencies sum up why so many small business start-ups fail. We knew if we could give small businesses expertise in these areas, and if the new entrepreneurs took advantage of what we were offering, their ability to survive past that fourth year grew exponentially. New small business owners need to invest in themselves and avail themselves of any programs that are available locally or on the Internet for free or at almost no cost. "I'm too busy," is what we usually heard from new small business owners. However, they would have had plenty of time on their hands if their new businesses shut the doors a year or two down the road.

Look at it this way. Say the new small business owner is like the man who has only an old, rusty saw to cut a path through a rough thicket. It's backbreaking work, a struggle, and certainly no fun. If only this man had a shiny, new, sharp saw. He could cut that path—to success—in no time. But like the small business owner who won't stop to get the skills he or she needs and is deficient in, the man cutting through that thicket has no time to stop wielding that rusty, old saw. If he took the time to get the saw sharpened—to acquire the education and technical assistance—cutting his way through the rough thicket would be much easier.

People usually say they want to be in business for themselves because they perceive it to be glamorous. They say, "Oh, I'll be able to take off all the time I want, go on long vacations, make lots of money, and not have to answer to anyone but myself." But the truth of the matter is most people who own small businesses work longer hours than those employed by others. They are not working 40 hours a week; it's usually closer to 60 hours or 80 hours a week. They can take a vacation, but they often choose not to because they don't want to leave their business. If they are making money, they usually put it right back into the business, so they're not living extravagantly.

But those small business owners who are passionate about what they do will tell you there is nothing they would rather do. They love what they are doing. Yes, it's challenging; yes, it's difficult, but they wouldn't have it any other way. That is reflective of the mind-set of people who are successful at running a small business. They are almost grateful they get to do this; they are not complaining. There are business owners who say, "I'd pay to do this—they don't have to pay me; I would pay them."

I have quite literally spent my whole life in and around small business. My father was an entrepreneur, starting numerous small businesses. I worked in many of them. As I got older, I ran some of his businesses. I have worked in a corporate environment providing services for small businesses, and I have owned and operated small businesses. For more than five years, as head of the SBA, I was in charge of delivering programs and services to small businesses in the United States, formulating government policy toward small business, and implementing that policy.

This lifetime in and around many different kinds of small businesses—some very successful, some less so—has given me insight about why some succeed, why some fail, and what an entrepreneur needs to do to best ensure that a good idea or good product will be translated into a successful business.

Along the road, I have met thousands of very successful small business people. Some have grown their businesses from the most humble of beginnings into corporate giants whose names are household words and whose operations are integral parts of the national economy. Other successful entrepreneurs I know well may not be instantly recognizable, but each is successful by any standard and quite often well beyond his or her dreams.

In the pages that follow, I have called on many of these successful entrepreneurs to share their stories and their secrets of success. Many have learned lessons the hard way; most have overcome daunting obstacles. Now they would like to help you avoid these pitfalls so you too can enjoy the kind of success they have enjoyed.

I like to say that everything I learned about small business I learned in a Mexican restaurant. My father, Hector Barreto Sr., and my mother Mary Louise were immigrants from Guadalajara, Mexico. My father used to tell me that from his earliest memories he was either working in a business or owning a business. When he was in his early twenties, he bought and sold cattle in Jalisco State in central Mexico—Mexico's Wild West with its ranches, horses, and cattle. He ran into some difficult times, so he decided to join some family members in the United States, work for a while, save some money, and then go back.

My father came to the United States on a work visa, which were plentiful in those days. His relatives were in Kansas City. He had no real idea where that was except that it was in the center of the United States.

In the beginning, the only jobs my father could get were labor-intensive jobs; for instance, working on the railroad pounding spikes into the ground or picking potatoes for 50 cents an hour in rural Missouri. He worked at a meatpacking house cleaning out stalls. Eventually, he became the janitor at the small Catholic school that I would later attend.

My dad always said those jobs were a means to an end, something temporary until he could do what he really wanted to do, which was to be his own boss. He eventually fulfilled that dream and probably did much more than he had ever dreamed possible.

The first business my father started was a Mexican restaurant. He chose that, as many people do, because the entry cost was low; he and my mom, who was a great cook, knew how to make Mexican food, so he felt it would be an easy business to get into.

In the late 1950s, being in the Mexican food business in Kansas City was really cutting edge. No one knew what a taco, an enchilada, or a burrito was. My parents made a go of it despite not having any formal training in running a restaurant. Our family all worked together, and eventually that one restaurant led to two, and two led to three. First there was Mexico Lindo, then Chico's, and later on Casa Blanca (White House)—which came at a time when my father helped found the U.S.-Hispanic Chamber of Commerce and got involved as an advisor to President Ronald Reagan.

It was my father who started these businesses—he was a visionary—but it was my mom who actually ran them on a day-to-day basis. My dad was constantly away making contacts or putting deals together.

As so often happens with entrepreneurs, my parents' business evolved. People came into the restaurants, liked the food, and asked my dad if he could get this type of food for them to make at home. This led him to start a small import-export business. We imported food and produced other foodstuffs, and eventually Mexican furniture and Mexican tiles like those in our restaurant decorations because diners would ask where they could buy them for their homes.

In the beginning, his method of importing was to drive a truck into Mexico, fill it up with merchandise, and drive it back to Kansas City. He often drove straight through with maybe a few hours sleep by the side of the interstate. It was a long drive and certainly not very efficient. As the business grew, it became too much. He had to hire trucks and drivers to make the trips, and then as it grew further, he started to ship by railcar.

My dad used to say it wasn't enough that he personally be successful; he wanted to help others. He wanted to join a business organization with other Hispanic businesses because at the time there were a number of Hispanic businesses in Kansas City. But there was no such organization to join, so my father started his own. With some other Hispanic businessmen, my father helped start the Kansas City Hispanic Chamber of Commerce. It started small but that Chamber grew as more and more Hispanic businesses started locally. Similarly, when he later wanted to join a national organization and found that it didn't exist, my father started reaching out to Hispanic business leaders across the country and that led to the start of the U.S. Hispanic Chamber of Commerce.

This was during a time when there were not that many Hispanic-owned businesses in the United States. Today, there are over two million U.S. Hispanic-owned businesses that generate revenues in excess of $300 billion, and those numbers are increasing rapidly. Hispanic-owned businesses are the fastest growing segment of small business, with some economists predicting a tidal wave of growth, such as their number doubling every five years over the next several decades as Hispanic-owned businesses become even more important to the U.S. economy.

It was not so back then. But my father was a visionary; he could see the future. The U.S. Hispanic Chamber has grown and developed a national reputation: it even has a national television show every Sunday. It is conceivable that within a decade there will be eight million Hispanic-owned businesses in this country. It is not a small, niche market any more.

My father had an interest in politics. He was involved with the Reagan campaign and later was involved in President Reagan's transition from the White House. Then he became involved with George H. W. Bush, in his campaign and administration. He became an American citizen—one of his proudest moments—because he felt that was not only logical but important now that he was working within the American political system.

When my father was getting involved politically, I was just starting college. At the same time, he started the third restaurant— Casa Blanca—on the west side of Kansas City that was not near where we lived, nor was it near the other two restaurants.

Just as Casa Blanca was opening, my father was called back to Washington, DC, to advise President Reagan on a full-time basis. He said, "Hector Jr., this restaurant is now your responsibility." So while I was trying to go to college, I was suddenly a 19-year-old running a small business.

Fortunately, I had been working in the family restaurants for years. I had started waiting tables when I was nine, but this time I was the boss. I had no experience opening a restaurant or running one myself, and I was scared to death I wouldn't make it and I would let my folks down. They weren't worried though; they had total confidence—that's just how our family was. My father handed me the keys to the building and said, "Don't worry, you'll learn." That's how I got my first experience running a small business.

In our family, it was assumed that everyone would accept responsibility. The only failure was not giving it your best, of not trying. That is a lesson for all entrepreneurs. They need to be able to project themselves forward into an opportunity, even when they don't know how it's going to turn out. It's a question of faith, of confidence, of will, and of being relentless.

It was somewhat overwhelming trying to open a new business and take a full class schedule in college, but I persevered. We had three restaurants, but, even though they shared the common thread of serving Mexican food, all three were very different. They had different menus, different chefs, different purveyors and suppliers, and different policies.

After college, I left the restaurant—which was going strong—and moved to Texas where I worked as an area manager for the Miller Brewing Company and dealt with a wide range of beer distributors and small businesses—bars, restaurants, convenience stores, and liquor stores. It was quite a change working for a large corporation after working in the family business, but I came in contact with small business owners on a daily basis and saw what made some very successful, while others struggled.

Working for a big company had always appealed to me, and there were certainly many advantages to it: There was training, job security, and all the trappings of success, but I literally felt trapped; I missed working for myself, creating something from scratch. It was my entrepreneurial genes coming out. So I moved to California to join a boyhood friend who had moved there and who had gotten involved in the insurance and financial services industry. He recruited me away from Miller Brewing to come to the West Coast to pursue my entrepreneurial dreams by helping him build his business.

It sounded like an exciting opportunity, but if I had known everything that was going to happen before I made the decision, I might have been a little more hesitant before jumping in. In hindsight,

I'm glad I went to California because it helped me accomplish so many of my goals. But at the time, it was difficult moving from the protection and shelter of a large corporation with its benefits and great salary and other perks and going into a business I really didn't know anything about. Starting over again from scratch is a very sobering experience, regardless of your age, but especially when you are 26 years old.

In the beginning, I was primarily selling life insurance, one-on-one. Then I started selling health insurance to the same individuals. As their businesses grew and they added employees, I sold insurance to their employees. Later, the business began to grow and change; it evolved. And like my father branching out into the import and export business, I went from insurance into a broader financial services operation, working with small business owners on their various financial needs and financial planning.

This led to acquiring a securities broker-dealer license and starting my own broker-dealer firm, one of the few Hispanic-owned firms of its kind in the country. It was challenging for me to obtain the state and federal licenses and get the business off the ground.

I was also involved with the Latin Business Association and, over 15 years, worked from being a member to serving on committees to chairing large events. Eventually, I was elected to the board, ultimately becoming the vice chairman and then the board chairman. At the time, it was the largest Hispanic business organization on the West Coast and one of the largest in the country.

We had then-Governor of Texas George W. Bush speak to us at a luncheon for 3,000 of our members. I met him there for the first time, and he eventually asked me to get involved with his presidential campaign. I was involved as a co-chairman in California and became a surrogate for him speaking around the country. I spoke at the national GOP convention and worked closely with him through the campaign period. He understood my background with small business and, after the election, personally asked me to head the SBA.

It was a huge honor, but totally unexpected. I was minding my own business quite literally: It was growing and I was feeling the initial benefits of real success. I had to give the request considerable thought because a move to Washington was going to be at considerable cost, both financially and emotionally. I had to move a very young family across the country and ask my wife to make sacrifices, but anytime the president of the United States asks you to serve your country, it's a huge honor. I felt, and still feel, an important obligation to repay what this country has done for my family. The president's faith in me, and the opportunity he gave me, is something I'll always be grateful for and never forget.

I ended up being the second longest-serving SBA administrator—serving five-plus years while the average tenure of an SBA administrator over the 53-year history of the agency has been 18 months.

My time as head of the SBA allowed me to constantly travel around the country, meeting with small business owners in every state multiple times. I spent countless hours with SBA professionals who have spent their careers helping small business owners succeed. We had roundtables and regional events where I would hear firsthand the stories of small business success. The thousands of business owners I met, who took the time to share with me their stories of accomplishments, allowed me to earn a very practical "PhD"—if you will—in small business success.

Talking with these countless small business owners, and determining what they needed to help them grow their businesses, led me to help develop the president's Small Business Agenda with emphases ranging from better sources of capital for small business to better availability of procurement opportunities, lower taxes and regulation, less litigation, and most important—small businesses's number one concern—some relief from the healthcare crisis and the ever-escalating cost of insurance, both for them and their families personally and for their employees.

I'm proud that access to capital for small businesses doubled during my tenure at the SBA. When I arrived, the SBA was guaranteeing about $9 billion in loans annually. When I left, we had increased that amount to $20 billion and, just as important, a third of that was loans to the emerging market, businesses owned by minorities and women. When I arrived, we were training about a million small business owners a year. When I left, that number had doubled to two million small business owners a year. When I arrived, the federal government was providing small business about $50 billion in contracts annually; when I left, it provided $80 billion in contracts thanks to the cooperative efforts among those of us in government (especially the incredible team at the SBA), the private sector, and countless volunteers. It was an honor to serve with them at a time of incredible transformation within the SBA and our country, especially after the terrorist attacks of 9/11.

Late in 2005, I was invited to become the chairman of and to help lead the Latino Coalition—one of the nation's most dynamic Hispanic organizations—so I asked the president to allow me to leave the SBA. He asked me to stay until a replacement could be found, which turned out to be in July 2006. Now I am at the Latino Coalition, working with the new presidential administration in Mexico to help them better understand the United States, and I've joined the boards of several companies. I'm also advising some major companies how best to reach the small business market, and I've begun to aggressively pursue the entrepreneurial interests that I had put on hold until I had completed my years of government service. I am part of a group that is in the process of opening a bank in booming Las Vegas, Nevada.

Along with my work at the Latino Coalition, one of the most exciting things I am presently doing is acting as chairman of a privatized and expanded program I helped start: Business Matchmaking is one of the proudest achievements of my five years at the helm of the SBA. The idea, which I originally started when I headed the Latin Business Association in California, was to bring together motivated buyers and qualified sellers. The buyers were motivated because they wanted to do business with small business; the sellers were qualified because we had pretrained, educated, and informed them how to do business with big business and the government. When I got to the SBA, I quickly realized that, while the agency took its traditional role of helping provide capital and training for small business owners seriously, a key part of the equation of success—helping them secure new business—was lacking. This gap could definitely be filled with government help, so we formed a unique public/private partnership with the help of visionary private sector colleagues Chuck Ashman and Diane Kegley and forward-looking companies such as Hewlett-Packard, American Airlines, and Aflac. We started Business Matchmaking more than three years ago.

For a small business to succeed, it needs *know-how* but it also needs to know who. It doesn't need a handout, but a helping hand. Small business wants the exact same thing that big business wants—more business.

To help accomplish this, we developed the Business Match-making concept—think speed dating for the small business. In large gatherings across the country, we brought together purchasing officials from government agencies—federal, state, and local—and some of the United States's biggest corporations and matched their needs with the offerings of thousands of small businesses. We match the small businesses with the buyers of the exact products they are offering in a series of 15-minute meetings. Typically, at a Business Matchmaking session, we have had 300 to 500 small business owners meeting with the procurement people from 200 corporations and governmental agencies in 2,000-plus one-on-one meetings.

Obviously, you are not going to sell your product in 15 minutes (although on a few occasions I have seen it happen), but the small business owner is going to be able to begin a relationship with that government agency or corporation, to get the access he or she has difficulty in achieving. It transforms what is often a difficult and, some say, humiliating pursuit. The small business owner can get a better understanding of the process the agency or company uses to acquire goods and services and its specific needs, and learn how to fit into that process. The short meeting, in turn, gives the procurement official the ability to put a face together with future phone or Internet contacts and it gives him or her a more direct feel for whom their corporation may be dealing with in the future. A synergy often develops that will lead to future business.

The Business Matchmaking sessions also have given us the opportunity to help thousands of small business owners get ready to do business with large corporations. These sessions give the small business owner access to the buyers and the decision makers who give out contracts that he probably could not get on his own.

We train the small business owner in what to expect, how to market his company, and most important about the processes he will have to be involved in to begin selling on perhaps a broader basis then he has experienced before. This costs the small business owner nothing but his time and commitment.

The results have been nothing short of phenomenal. In three years, we have facilitated over 50,000 Business Matchmaking appointments. These appointments have led to over $1 billion in contracts for the small businesses who first made contact with a future customer at Business Matchmaking. It's not something that happens instantly; typically, first contracts are obtained three to six months after that initial meeting.

Now, through the establishment of a new private sector company, Small Business Matchmaking, the concept is going to be broadened even further; over the coming years, we are going to be able to expose small businesses to more and even greater opportunities.

Over my more than five years heading the SBA, I met with many extremely successful small business owners; they told me their stories and their secrets to success. In this book, I share many of those success stories and many of the insights I have gleaned over the years. Small business owners reflect the best of this country. They are the backbone of our economy, and I'm proud to be a part of this community.

What many of these successful small business owners have in common are their values, character, perseverance, faith, and goodwill to others—their employees, customers, the communities they come from, and their families. I hope to be able to articulate what makes them so special so you can emulate their success and learn from them.

We see many examples in the following pages. Among them are:

Thanh Quoc Lam—A Vietnamese refugee who fled in a leaky boat with only the shirt on his back in the closing days of the Vietnam War with just the possessions he could carry. He ended up moving to Hawaii; there he got into the bakery business, opened a French bakery, and eventually became the SBA's National Small Business Person of the Year in 2002. He told me the proudest thing that ever happened to him was becoming a U.S. citizen. He laughingly said, "Hector, it's only in America that a refugee who was running for his life could end up in Hawaii, start a French bakery in Chinatown, end up selling his products to the airlines and the largest hotels in the Islands, build such a successful business, and then meet the president of the United States in the White House."

Linda Alvarado—She started a construction company at a time when it was very unusual (actually, it still is) for a woman to be involved in the construction industry. Everybody told her she couldn't make it, that she was crazy, or they would ask where her husband was. She is now the head of one of the most successful construction companies in the United States. She is a part owner of the Colorado Rockies baseball team, sits on several corporate boards, and is a member of the SBA's Hall of Fame.

Earl Graves Sr.—An aide to Bobby Kennedy whose world seemed to come to an end the day Bobby Kennedy was killed in Los Angeles, he had an idea about going into business for himself. He went back to New York and started making the rounds of the banks, and every one of them slammed the door in his face when he put forth his idea of starting a financial magazine for the African American community. He finally got a loan from a bank that obtained an SBA guarantee so that it would get most of its money back if he failed. Earl Graves has gone on to become an incredible role model and his *Black Enterprise* magazine is a huge success by any standard. He now sits on several corporate boards and was one of the largest soft drink bottlers in the Mid-Atlantic region. He has been a great success and an indelible inspiration at whatever he has tried.

Tom Stemberg—He had an idea for an office supply company and started a company he called Staples that almost went out of business even before it got started when the store had a disastrous fire. It was through the efforts of his employees that he was able to reopen and, as he built the Staples empire, he has always had tremendous loyalty to the people who work for him. He has become a disciple of contingency planning because, as he told me, it's not a question of if problems are going to arise, but when, and if you are ready to face them.

It's been my experience in meeting thousands of successful small business owners that it's not where you start that's important, but where you end up. Many of the decisions these small business owners made, many of the challenges they faced and overcame, have allowed them to become greater successes than they ever imagined. Listening to them provides the fledgling entrepreneur with practical advice about how to start a business or how to take a business to the next level. Regardless of the type of business, or where that business is in terms of its growth, others have gone before you and have experienced what you are experiencing. It is critical to learn from them—and it will be critical for those who come next to learn from you.

If you can teach a small business owner something that he or she doesn't know but that is critical to the growth of the business or that allows him or her to avoid a critical mistake, you have helped put that person on the road to success.

That is what I am endeavoring to do in this book. Over the years, many successful small business owners have helped me; now, I hope to give some of that help back.

I believe businesses of all types are evolutionary. No one starts out as a household name listed on the Fortune 500. Most people start at the bottom and work their way up. No two businesses are exactly the same. They bring very different resources or skill sets to their enterprise. In writing this book, I have attempted to provide subject matter that would be relevant to multiple audiences. Many people who read this book are just beginning as small business owners and need basic information that they can utilize immediately in their businesses.

Others are entrepreneurs who have been at it for a while and maybe have experienced success already, but who are committed to taking their business to the next level. These businesses have already mastered the basics, but they need some critical advice to overcome a challenge or to learn from someone who has already achieved what they are attempting to accomplish.

Finally, some may not even be close to being in business, but they are trying to decide if they want to be or should be in business for themselves. They may be going through a process of determining if this is right for them. They may say, "I didn't know that or I never thought about that." Maybe a lightbulb will go off and it will help them make the best decision.

At the end of the day, each person who invests time reading this book—whether that is someone just starting out or contemplating his own business or someone at a new stage of growth of his business, even if he thinks of himself as an experienced entrepreneur looking for a new challenge or perhaps an exit strategy—should expect to receive something relevant from what follows.

I am reminded of the process someone goes through when making an important investment. If you're working with an expert or financial services professional, he or she determines your objectives and risk tolerance because many people believe they are more knowledgeable and more of a risk taker than they probably really are. By going through a simple set of questions or hypothetical situations with the financial planner, you can get a very clear take on what the best course of action is for you. By imagining what could happen, pro and con, you are in a much better position to make a good decision. It's similar when making important decisions about your small business.

Many people think they should be their own boss and have their own business because it seems glamorous to be their own boss, potentially make lots of money, and be totally independent, but the truth is often very different: You'll work harder than you ever worked; you probably won't make any real money for much longer than you expected; and, as for freedom, you will devote all your free time to this new dependent called *your small business.* Reality has a way of confronting you in ways you never imagined or expected. Don't get me wrong. I know from personal experience the incredible opportunities and rewards that being in business for yourself can provide you and your family. I also know it won't be easy. Most people want to work for themselves, but many should not.

So let's begin our journey.

II | Principles of Success

2

Plan—Don't Just Wing It

When we look across the spectrum at businesses that succeed and those that, regretfully, fail, we are always on the lookout for common threads. What is it about those that make it, and make it big, that is often absent from those that don't make it? Look at enough businesses and one answer pops out—early planning.

You have come up with that killer idea for a product or service, one that you are sure there is a market for and one that you're sure will make you rich. You are now determined to start that business and be off on the road to riches.

What next? Mitchell Rubinson, a Miami-based entrepreneur who has had a 30-year string of business successes, has a formula: "I have a very simple entrepreneurial system: Think it, plan it, do it. Don't waste time, focus on what it is, think about it, plan it, and execute it."

The key word in his personal formula is *plan*.

As you begin to tell others of your idea, you get the same questions from almost everyone you speak with who you think has any expertise in business— "Do you have a business plan?" "Have you written a business plan?" "You're going to need a business plan." You will hear some variation of these questions wherever you turn.

At the Small Business Administration (SBA), we stressed the necessity of planning as a starting point for developing a viable business. Essentially, a business plan is a road map to success, one that gives the entrepreneur a sense of direction. It's greatest value is to early on give the new small business owner the opportunity to identify the strengths and weaknesses of a proposed new business and the ability to first fail on paper before more time and capital are expended and the effects of failure are so much greater.

But what exactly are we talking about when we talk about a *business plan*? Many new entrepreneurs think of it as a document that is needed to take to a bank to get a loan, or something to give to potential investors. That is one type of business plan, but not necessarily something that is needed initially. That is what might be called an *external plan,* one that is developed to be seen by potential funders or suppliers of the new business.

Much more important is a *start-up plan* that lays out the rationale for undertaking the proposed new business and defines the steps that must be taken in launching the new business. It should describe the product or service to be offered, analyze the potential market, do some forecasting, lay out a strategy, set up goals and milestones, and talk about a management team. It should include some basic financial analysis including sales projections, profit and loss statements, cash flow statements, and probably an initial balance sheet. This start–up plan is an internal document and not one meant for outside dissemination. It is primarily for your use. It should define your business and identify your goals.

Okay, so you understand that you need such a plan. Don't wait! Get on with it. You might not yet know all the financial details, or even be able to forecast what you'll need and what your sales and income is likely to be at any point; you're not ready to go out to a bank or to an angel investor, but that does not mean you do not need a plan.

One place to start is with something called a SWOT exercise— Strengths, Weaknesses, Opportunities, and Threats. It is simply brainstorming—an organized way of starting to look at your business idea. You should be thinking about:

- What service or product does your business provide and what needs does it fill?
- Who are the potential customers for your product or service and why will they purchase it from you?
- How will you reach your potential customers?
- Where will you get the financial resources to start your business?

My friend Louis Barajas is one of the smartest financial planners I know. Over the years, he has worked with many small business owners, mostly successful small business owners, but more than a few who have failed or whose businesses never reached the level they had hoped. Over the years, Louis has developed valuable insights as to what separates the successful small businesses from those that fall short or, even worse, those that fail altogether.

One of his most valuable pieces of advice is: "Your business is your business, not just your product or service."* He means that it takes more than a good idea—or even a great idea—or more than a great product or service to make a successful small business. Rather, you can start with a great idea or a great product or service and if you can develop an infrastructure to surround that great idea, a way to market and deliver that product or service to your intended audience, then and only then will you have the hope of running a really successful small business.

"Just because you know how to do something," Barajas says, "doesn't mean you know how to run a business. You can have the greatest product or service in the world, but unless you have created a business to support that product or service, you're not going to be around for very long."

Barajas advises that you need to have a *business blueprint* by which to run a successful small business. This differs from a business

---

*This idea and much more are contained in his new book *Small Business, Big Life: Five Steps to Creating a Great Life with Your Own Small Business* (Nashville, TN: Thomas Nelson, 2007).

plan, which is essentially a document whose central purpose is to help attract financing or a loan. That kind of plan, Barajas goes on to say, is not a guide for running a business. A business blueprint identifies all the major functions and tasks required to run a business.

I've know small business owners who seem almost adverse to sitting down and drafting a blueprint defining what they will need to do to run their business. They might do a formal business plan because it is something a lender demands, but it will be limited to financial matters. Others might do something approaching Barajas's idea of a business blueprint, but they will turn it into a checklist and will simply check this box or that box, and then move on to the next unchecked box.

There certainly is some level of value in this; at least it's better than no list at all. Moreover, the exercise of developing this checklist might tell the new business owners the things they need to learn. But essentially it still misses the point. The plan should be a living document. No business, at least no successful business, remains static. A business changes as it grows. The business plan or blueprint must change as the business evolves and changes. If it does, then it's a valuable exercise, not simply some kind of "make-work" effort, and one that will actually help an entrepreneur on the road to success.

We briefly met Linda Alvarado in Chapter 1, and we will hear from her at length later in this book. She is an incredibly successful entrepreneur who has gone from starting a small construction subcontracting firm—cutting curbs and pouring sidewalks—to owning a general contracting organization with an international reach that builds major public and private projects.

She believes strongly that an entrepreneur who is starting must have a blueprint:

> You have to have a sense of direction and goals. More than that, you have to have a sense of how you're going to get there. I call it a blueprint. There is no perfect blueprint; it always changes. There has to be a sense of commitment about what you're going to do. The how can change while you're trying to achieve a sense of balance. It's not just about volumes and profits and stature, you need a sense of balance with your family and your community.

Her thoughts are echoed by LuLu Sobrino, who we will meet at length in Chapter 3, who says:

> Do research. Spend your money there before you put it in a business, why, because I hate to see businesses fail for lack of research. You have to have a business plan and that business plan has to have on paper all kinds of scenarios before you put money in a business. You need a prudent plan of action.

My good friends at SCORE, "Counselors to America's Small Business," whose work you will see throughout this book and who we will meet at length in a later chapter, counsel hundreds of thousands of small business owners and prospective small business owners each year.

SCORE counselors are big believers in planning and the very early drafting of plans by anyone considering starting a business. "A business plan provides you with a comprehensive, detailed overview of all the aspects of your business," SCORE says. "This overview is the skeleton of your business—the underlying structure that provides the basis of your entire operation. Prepared in advance, a business plan allows you to review the pros and cons of your proposed business before you make a financial and emotional commitment to it."

SCORE has synthesized its many years of experience into some invaluable aides and teaching tools. One of the best is a booklet—"How to Really Start Your Own Business"—which all persons they counsel are given early in the process. The booklet is available at any of the 380 SCORE offices nationwide.

Have you ever heard the term "elevator pitch?" It's often used in a sales or marketing context. You are in business and for months you have been trying to get in front of a key executive to present your business so you can make a much needed sale. Now you are at a convention and you step onto an elevator and there he or she is. It's your golden opportunity to present your business or idea and you have until the elevator reaches the lobby to do so. You have to summarize your company and its product or service, and make it interesting, probably in a minute or less. This is an "elevator pitch."

Along those same lines, SCORE believes that almost as a starting point to any planning, you need to be able to break your idea down into its essence and suggests that you draft a document that includes the following:

1. Summarize your business idea in 50 words or less.
2. Where did your idea originate (from a specific experience, industry observation, a sudden inspiration)?
3. If your idea is for a new product or service, describe how you expect to get it accepted in the market.
4. If your idea is for an improvement or variation of an existing product or service, describe why consumers will use it instead of what is already available.
5. Describe your market niche in 50 words or less.
6. List at least three qualifications that you have that will allow you to pursue a business in this market niche (work experience, education, research, reputation, etc.).
7. What are your two most important personal goals for the next five years (independence, visibility, income, personal satisfaction, etc.)?
8. How will this business help you achieve those personal goals?
9. List and describe briefly the two most significant barriers to expect while launching and operating your business.
10. Explain how you expect to overcome these challenges.

You should do it as a valuable exercise and above all you should not exceed the word limits that were given.

Robert d'Agostino, is a long-time SCORE counselor in Westchester County, outside New York City. Bob is one of the very best, and he specializes in planning and helping both new and growing businesses get the kind of financing they need to put them on solid footing.

He is a long-time advocate of planning, and not just to create a document that can be used in applying for a loan. From long experience, he believes that planning is absolutely necessary right from the start for any business.

"I tell them an idea is great, but the idea is in your head, it's between your ears, and you can't sell an idea that's in your brain," he says as he explains the process he uses when counseling a new entrepreneur:

You have to convert the idea into a goal, and then the goal has to be transferred into a written document called a business plan, and then the business plan is turned into an action plan. So it starts with a dream, the dream is converted into a goal, the goal into a written plan, the written plan is put into an action plan, then the fourth step is jumping off the diving board so to speak and doing it.

Sometimes the clients we have had do very well up until the fourth step, and they can't quite turn it into action. They get scared, or they get hesitant, or they're afraid of risk, whatever the reason happens to be, or pressure from a family member, and they go to that final step and they don't jump, they don't jump off that board.

How important is planning? Both entrepreneurs who have made it big and academics who have studied the relationship between business planning for a start-up and the eventual success or failure of those ventures say it is critical.

One of the most interesting studies I have seen was done by Professor Frédéric Delmar of the Center for Entrepreneurship and Business Creation, Stockholm School of Economics, and Professor Scott Shane of Case Western Reserve University's Weatherhead School of Management.[*]

They looked at a random sample of 223 new ventures started over a period of 30 months. Looking at those that made it, and those that didn't, they came to three conclusions:

1. Business planning reduces the hazard of new venture disbanding;
2. Business planning facilitates product development in new ventures; and
3. Business planning facilitates venture-organizing activity in new ventures. . . . Ultimately, by helping firm founders to make decisions, business planning increases the chance of venture survival, accelerating product development and venture organizing.

If you've eaten any frozen Mexican food at home, the chances are pretty good that it was made by Ruiz Foods. "It was my dad's

[*]"Does Business Planning Facilitate the Development of New Ventures?" *Strategic Management Journal*, December 2003, pp. 1165–1185.

idea," Fred Ruiz, the company's president, remembers. "My dad has always been an entrepreneur and he had this idea of making frozen Mexican food. My family was originally from Mexico, we've been in the United States for about 80 years. When I got out of college, my dad came to me with the idea of frozen Mexican food. This was back in 1963. He asked if I wanted to be his partner. I wasn't married, and I was still living at home, so I thought why not."

Ruiz Foods started out as a very small business, not so much "mom and pop" as a "pop and son" operation—Ruiz and Son, if you will. But in 43 years, it has grown very large.

"My dad had this warehouse business, so we took a small part of the warehouse and made it into a little kitchen, and we took my mom's kitchen utensils and her mixer and some of her pots and pans, and a small freezer, and that's how Ruiz Foods started.

"Today, we have three plants, two in California and one in Texas, and we have over a half-million square feet of manufacturing and warehouse space, and we have over 2,500 employees. We now have a brand, Monterey, that's well known, number one in the United States. In the area of frozen Mexican food, we're competing with many companies both large and small, but 20 cents out of every dollar spent for frozen Mexican food is spent with us. We manufacture over four million burritos a day, and with Mexican food becoming more and more popular across the United States, we continue to grow rapidly. We're right at a half-million dollars a year in sales."

As with many start-ups, the Ruiz's, father and son, did very little planning when they started up. They just sort of let things happen.

"It was probably not the best way to start a business, but when my dad and I started this frozen Mexican food business, we really didn't sit down and draw up a business plan. We didn't do marketing studies to try to look at the size of the market, but my dad was already very involved in the food business, and he believed that there was a growing market for frozen Mexican food. He and my uncles had a tortilla company and he knew from the fact that that company was continually growing, that the market for Mexican food in the United States was also growing."

This seat-of-the-pants approach got them through the early days, as it does with many small businesses, but the lack of planning eventually caught up with them, and suddenly they were faced with a crisis.

"When we had a small facility, it was operated under state meat inspection rules. Then the state decided to get out of the inspection business and turn it over to the federal government, the U.S. Department of Agriculture (USDA).

"The USDA came into our plant with a very different set of rules and regulations. They told us we were producing too much product for the size of our plant, and they said we had three choices: cut back, expand the existing facility, or build a new facility. That challenge took us to a whole new level as a business. What we ended up doing was building a new facility, and we used an SBA loan to fund the new construction.

"What I learned in this process was that we needed to do better planning. Some people came in and gave us help and for the first time we developed a formal business plan. This gave us more focus and a better understanding of how to run a business. The bottom line was we got the loan, we had a plan, and we went from a 2,500-square-foot facility to a 11,000-square-foot facility, which was a huge jump in terms of size and complexity.

"That whole experience, working with finances and with a more formalized planning process, was a very positive experience for me and for the company. In the long run, it made a huge difference both for me and for the company."

The lesson to be learned here is not only the need for planning initially, but the need to constantly revise any business plan.

Meet Steve Leveen, who with his wife Lori operates the Levenger Corporation, a high-end retailer of leather goods and "tools for the serious reader," a business they built starting in their garage. We look more in depth at his company in Chapter 6, but he has an interesting take on planning and starting a business.

"When I talk with students, I have a little talk that I call 'The Unlikely Entrepreneur' because my background was unlikely for becoming an entrepreneur," he says with a laugh referring to the fact that his undergraduate degree is a BA in biology from the University of California, San Diego, and his master's and doctoral degrees are in sociology from Cornell University.

"I give them a number of lessons I learned along the way, in the hopes that they might be relevant for them," he says of his appearances before groups of business students. "One of those lessons is 'Begin Before You're Ready.' What I mean by that is while it's important to do planning before you start a business, and I also believe strongly in business plans, there comes a point where you just have to take the plunge and start trying to sell your wares or provide your service and go through the basic steps of getting paid for it, paying your suppliers, and starting down the road to a profit and loss statement. I can't guarantee you what you'll learn when you do this, but I can guarantee that your learning is going to increase at a rapid pace once you actually start in business.

"Business planning, I believe, becomes more important as the business matures because, in the early phases, while writing a business plan before the business starts is a useful and worthwhile exercise, it can only take you so far. You have to take the leap of faith that you have a viable business and just get started.

"Almost certainly, your business will change from what you thought initially. You just don't know how, and you won't know how by sitting back in your armchair and trying to figure it out. Business is a participation sport, not a spectator sport."

In this book, I am not going to tell you how to write a business plan, or even in any detail what should go into it or how it should be presented. Help in this regard is abundantly available. There are literally dozens of places on the Web where you can get detailed help. There are computer programs you can buy that will do the job for you nicely. And, of course, as I have indicated, you can walk into any SCORE or Small Business Development Center (SBDC) office and either take a class or get one-on-one help in drafting your plan.

But all too often, I fear, in writing a business plan the end—having a nice-looking written plan—is seen as the end-all and be-all. Go to the Internet and you will find dozens, if not hundreds, of experienced consultants who stand ready—for a fee (and at times a very healthy fee) to write your business plan for you. I think all this misses the point completely.

Without meaning to get too Zen, drafting an initial business blueprint or business plan—the process itself—is much more important than the finished product. It is through the process that you can come to grips with exactly what it is you are trying to do and what strengths you can bring to bear. You can come face to face with the challenges you will have to face and what you will need to do to meet those challenges. The end result of the exercise should not simply be a "pretty document," or even a document that might result in a loan or an investment, but a new level of understanding of what it is going to take to launch the new business, or even if it is wise to go forward.

Writing a plan is *not* an end in itself. It is a necessary step and its value rests on the implementation of the plan. The plan is not a *static* document—it is organic. The day you begin implementing it, it becomes dated. Real-world experience will necessitate constant changing and updating to the point where the original plan may be all but unrecognizable.

One of the greatest benefits of a plan is that it sets goals. But once a goal is reached, it should become simply a waypoint toward the next goal.

SCORE lists three reasons for an entrepreneur starting out to draft a plan:

1. The process of creating a business plan forces you to take an objective, critical, and unemotional look at your business prior to and after its inception.
2. It is an operating tool that will help you manage your business and ensure its success.
3. It will communicate your ideas to others and provide the basis for financing proposals.

As you can see their primary reason is the process.

One man who learned this lesson well was Al Frink, who served in the Bush administration at the same time I did. As assistant secretary for manufacturing and services, International Trade Administration of the U.S. Department of Commerce, Frink was the chief advocate for the U.S. manufacturing and service sectors within the federal government and brought 30 years of private-sector experience to the job. As a small business executive, Frink built an internationally recognized carpet manufacturing company, Fabrica International, a carpet manufacturer from Orange County, California.

Frink cofounded Fabrica in 1974 with a $100,000 SBA loan. Fabrica develops, manufactures, and sells high-end luxury carpets and rugs to retailers, interior designers, furniture stores, and other markets and is considered the best in class. The company, which started with five employees, now has more than 400 employees and has never experienced major layoffs. Within the carpet industry, Fabrica distinguished itself through innovation and quality products. All of Fabrica's operations—including manufacturing and distribution—are located in the United States.

"I started out in retail sales and the door was opened for me to go to work for a carpet manufacturing company in southern California at the age of 23," Frink remembers. "At that time, most of the sales reps I was competing with were old enough to be my father. The economy was bad and the company I was working for was not doing well, but they were able to get a loan and save their business. Although I didn't realize it at the time, with a salesforce of eight people, I was accounting for one-third of the company's sales. I was promoted to sales manager when I was 26. I was able to recognize other good salespeople and that allowed me to build a sales team that was the envy of the industry. Many of the people I hired in those days went on to run their own companies very successfully.

"I went to work for a carpet manufacturer that taught me the production end of the business, and after a year when we tried to buy the company from its owners, they decided they didn't need us, and we ended up on the streets unemployed.

"We had learned a lot in that year, so we knew if we could get financing, we could start our own business. This was 1973 and the economy wasn't good. We met with a banker who suggested that we get an SBA-guaranteed loan. We went through the rigorous process and were able to get the funding.

"We felt we had found a niche—a higher quality and higher value product. Most of the carpet manufacturing companies in California at that time were trying to manufacture a lower quality product that they could sell at low cost. But we looked at it differently.

We thought to survive we needed to be a high-quality, high-end manufacturer. So we started Fabrica International in 1974.

"We were three young entrepreneurs and we had to thank the rigorous process that allowed us to get the SBA loan and that laid down the guidelines and forced on us the discipline to really manage our resources well. It forced us to develop a game plan and then to stick with it. The game plan or business plan that we had to develop to get the loan was probably more detailed and rigorous than it would have been had we developed one on our own. I credit the SBA guidelines that they put in place for us, that helped us get off to a good start, and that gave us a good framework on which to build. It forced us to plan and plan ahead, and that was so important to help us get to where we ended up."

The company was acquired by The Dixie Group in 2000.

"When we sold the company in the year 2000, we were doing about $47 million annually, and by the time the sale was final, after a long transition, we had gotten it up to about $60 million," Frink says. "The international market was 7 percent of our sales, but 14 percent of our profits. We had gone from 5 employees to about 450.

"Of the three of us who started as partners, I was the last man standing. My other partners had left over the years. We built something very special based on added value, based on finding unique niches in the market, and by producing a quality product."

I should also mention briefly another aspect of planning that might not occur to a new entrepreneur—contingency planning. Several sayings come to mind—"Whatever can go wrong, will go wrong" is one. "Expect the worse and you will never be disappointed" is another. I think you see where I am going with this.

Contingency planning is really nothing more than an exercise in trying to answer the question: "What would I do, if ?"

Even before a business opens its doors or launches its services, the owner must sit down, and perhaps with the help of a counselor, undertake to prepare a comprehensive list of the potentially serious incidents that could affect the normal operations of the business. This list should include all possible incidents no matter how remote the possibility might seem.

There are potentially quite a number of possibilities ranging from a fire or natural disaster to the failure of a key piece of equipment or system down to losing a key employee because of illness or resignation—and everything in between.

The next part of the exercise is to look at each possibility and in effect say, "If this happens, I will do thus and such." It can also mean—and in many instances this is even more important than planning how you will respond to a crisis—planning what you will do to *avoid* the crisis or to *mitigate its effect* should it occur.

One obvious step is to back up all data on your computer system every day. Talk to the experts and they will tell you back up, back up, back up until they sound like a broken record. But it is amazing how many companies do not and how many face lengthy and costly disasters.

Later you will meet at length Tom Stemberg who invented the concept of the office superstore and went from one Staples store to 1,900. He is almost fanatical on the subject of contingency planning. He can point to a very scary event, a fire in one of his two initial Staples stores, which could easily have put him out of business even before he got started.

He had done contingency planning, although not necessarily planning specifically how to respond to a potentially devastating fire, but to some major interruption of the normal business operation. So on that Saturday afternoon, as his dream almost burned to the ground, he had some definite ideas on how to respond. One thing was as simple as keeping an off-premises list of all employees with alternative ways of contacting them.

"By Saturday night, every one of our associates had come in and was working feverishly to get things cleaned up and get product from the other store so we could reopen. I truly believe contingency planning was vital to the survival of Staples."

Remember, even before you start out you need to remind yourself: "It's not a question of if, just when." You will encounter some kind of setback. It doesn't have to define you, unless you let it. Contingency plans are the key. We learned this during the 9/11 terrorist attacks and Hurricane Katrina—the two bookends of my tenure at the helm of the SBA. Those businesses that had a back up plan often were the only ones that could get back in business before they were completely crippled. Those who had not done the planning often never came back.

You know the old saying, "No business plans to fail, but most fail to plan." You know the statistics: 50 percent of small businesses will cease operations within four years. That is a huge loss to those businesses and their families and employees on a personal level. But it is also a huge loss for the U.S. economy and for our future economic prospects as a nation.

Another example of winging it happened when I first started in the insurance business. I struggled with being the most professional insurance and financial services agent possible. I'm not sure I ever fully committed to being in the industry from the outset, and that became a big challenge that I did not confront in the beginning because of my previous corporate management experience. I focused my attention on having the most accurate files. I focused on having an orderly office. I focused on adhering to best policies and procedures, and the truth is I wasn't going anywhere fast.

Being in the business was a struggle and not very much fun. After a year, I was really discouraged. I wasn't sure what was going wrong. I felt like I was working harder than ever putting in the hours and thinking and planning all the time. But the business was not forthcoming. Finally, I spoke with a senior agent and colleague who asked me an interesting and critical question: What is it that you do? I told him I was a professional insurance and financial services agent. "No, be more specific," he said. He asked me to tell him exactly what I did every hour of the day; so I proceeded to describe my daily schedule.

I told him that I arrived early in the morning. I went into my office and I opened up all my mail. I did all of my filing. I reviewed my plan for the day. I made a few phone calls. I spoke to some of the other agents in the office. I planned my week's activities. I made a few more phone calls. I tried to schedule a lunch with a prospective client, but often went to lunch by myself or with my colleagues. I would come back from lunch and try to meet with a client after lunch. Sometimes there weren't any appointments that day. At the end of the day, I would try to make some more phone calls, not all of them specifically business related. I volunteered my time to business organizations in the hopes of meeting potential clients. I would organize my office for the next day. Sometimes I would talk to clients I had already sold. I would do basically anything to keep myself busy, active, engaged in what I thought was running my business.

After I told him that, he said to me, "Why don't you just admit it?" I didn't understand. He said, "Why don't you just admit it—you're not in the insurance and financial services industry because successful insurance agents don't do what you do every day. They spend their time prospecting, closing cases, underwriting and delivering insurance policies. You spend very little of your time doing that, so why don't you stop kidding yourself and either make a real commitment to the business or do yourself and the industry a favor, and leave the industry."

I was floored. Now understand, this was someone I considered to be a friend. This was somebody who I looked up to. At first I felt insulted, but I also knew on a certain level that he was right. So I picked up whatever was left of my ego, and I made a commitment that I would engage in the insurance and financial services industry in a way that I had never done before. I could not accept failure. I was not going to return to my hometown and admit that I couldn't make it in my business after all those plans, after all of those dreams that I discussed with family and friends the past year.

And I began to stop doing all of the administrative work, all of the filing, all of the unnecessary phone calls, all of the wasted time, all of the conversations with friends and colleagues that led to no business, and I began to recommit myself to meeting as many potential clients as possible and helping them with their insurance needs.

Almost magically my business began to turn around. I was now starting to close accounts, starting to help people with their needs, and I never looked back from that point forward. I finally understood what I needed to do. And I did it.

I consider the conversation I had with this experienced insurance agent as a dose of tough love. He was being ruthlessly compassionate with me. He was being honest, and I needed that wake-up call. I think that most businesspeople need to have a similar conversation with themselves on a regular basis in order to keep themselves on track. Is what they're doing the thing that a successful person in their industry would do? You should emulate people who have gone before you, and professionals who are your peers and are having incredible success. You should find a way to duplicate those types of activities that truly lead to success and productivity.

I'm not suggesting to you for a moment that we should be like Simon Cowell on *American Idol* and embarrass and humiliate each other. But at the same time, I believe in honesty, openness, and truthfulness with one another. Not only does it save a lot of time, but it truly can help you to eliminate unproductive behavior. Often it is just a blind spot that we can't see in ourselves. We should be our worst critics and, when we need help, we should check our ego at the door and ask for help.

Linda Alvarado said that in the beginning when she lost a client, or prospective client, she was devastated by it. But later on, she made a commitment to resolve the situation for herself by going back to that client to ask why she hadn't gotten the business, and what she could have done differently to prevail. She would always learn something that would make her wiser and stronger for the next time. Often later, the client would call her back for a second opportunity because he or she was impressed by how she handled the initial setback.

I think that this type of discovery is a very healthy exercise. I also think it is something that not only makes us stronger, but it is a mark of true professionals who truly wants to improve their craft and wants to learn what they don't know so that they can improve their performance and eliminate negative and unproductive behavior. That's what it means to plan and not just wing it.

I like the saying: "Work your plan and plan your work." Commit to your plan. Put the blinders on and focus on the objectives to be accomplished. Often, this is not natural and becomes a learned behavior.

Finally, a plan won't do you any good if it is collecting dust on a shelf. A good plan should be a living, breathing document that you refer to frequently. Business is not static, and neither should your plan be. Think of it like a recipe that you always tinker with to keep improving the quality of the dish. Eventually you will have a fine meal to enjoy.

3

You Must Know What You Don't Know

It's clear that you must plan, both for the short term and for the long term. But how do you begin to formulate a plan and then put it down on paper? This is a major failing of many beginning and even veteran entrepreneurs. At the very start, every budding entrepreneur must realize what he or she doesn't know, and then figure out how to find the answers he or she needs.

Let me repeat for emphasis: You must know what you don't know. This means that you can't assume anything. You must ask yourself many questions. Most important, you must set out to get help and find the answers to your questions. Think of it as tinkering with the formula until it works perfectly.

One entrepreneur who faced this challenge and emerged as a success is Maria de Lourdes Sobrino, the founder and CEO of Lulu's Dessert Corporation. Established in 1982, Lulu's Dessert is ranked among the largest and fastest growing Hispanic-owned businesses in the United States. Hers is a classic tale of a product with great potential needing to have a business established around it.

41

Maria de Lourdes Sobrino—LuLu, as she is known to everyone—is a rare, born entrepreneur who had a great product/ idea, but then she had to turn it into a real business. I'll let her tell her own story:

> I was in my twenties when I started my first business in Mexico. My dad was a lawyer and his dad was a lawyer but for me it was just natural for me to have a business. I was the oldest of five and as the oldest I was expected to follow the steps of my father. But although I thought I could be a good lawyer, I wanted to be in business. So I asked my dad to allow me and I started a flower shop and then a second one. My mom used to help me. From there, I started my first company putting on conventions in Mexico. I would take groups from big U.S. companies like IBM or Xerox to Cancun. They wanted me to do the same thing in the United States, and I had a dream that one day I'd see what it was all about in the United States.

Her business began to shift to the well-to-do Mexicans who wanted to take family vacations at Disneyland or more adult sojourns in Las Vegas. Business boomed and LuLu thought the business could be better run from closer to the vacation spots where her clients were headed. So she opened an office in southern California after moving to the United States.

But it was 1982 and LuLu's timing was bad, the economy south of the border suddenly slipped into recession with the devaluation of the peso. Her client base of people looking for expensive U.S. vacations dried up overnight. This left her without a way to earn a living and wondering what to do:

> That's how being an entrepreneur really starts, with a dream. My dream was to come to the United States. After I opened my office, the economics changed, but I didn't want to go back to Mexico.

Things changed thanks to a shopping trip to get some ingredients for dessert:

> One Sunday, I wanted to buy the gelatin desserts that were traditional in Mexico, but I couldn't find any. So there it was. I had found my niche. As a consumer, I couldn't find something. So I decided to provide it. I used my mother's recipe and went to Mexico to do some research; I put in all my savings, opened this little 700-square-foot retail store in the city of Torrance, and from there faced challenges.

She had a better idea. She had a product—a three-layer gelatin in single-serving cups—and she knew how to make it. But she was only starting to learn what she didn't know:

> I didn't know anything about marketing. I didn't know anything about food. The first sales I made happened when I put my desserts—gelatins in little cups—in my car and went looking for first-generation Mexicans. I was the only company to have the gelatin desserts ready to eat, but I didn't know that. I had to educate myself on everything from the super-market buyers to the consumers. I left my product on a consignment basis in a supermarket saying, "Don't pay me until they sell." That gave the owner of the store the ability to take them with no risk. The first after-noon I did this, I got calls from the store owner saying, "Please come back, your gelatins are all gone, we've sold them all."
>
> So I was suddenly making 300 cups of gelatin a day and selling them that day all by myself because I didn't have any employees.

In 1983, with a number of local supermarkets now carrying her product, a buyer from a large regional grocery chain that had begun carrying her gelatins arranged to have her meet a food broker. He took on her product and introduced it to a much wider audience. It was an immediate hit, but success quickly brought problems. She simply could not meet demand from her mom-and-pop facility. She was only equipped to turn out gelatins that had to be quickly sold and consumed. She clearly needed a bigger production facility and a way to produce her product so that it would have a longer shelf life.

She went back for more education in food preparation and learned how to use preservatives. In 1985, she acquired a larger facility for production in nearby Gardena, California. As her out-lets grew, her payroll grew to keep pace; she needed capital. She learned how to draft a business plan with economic forecasts and was able to get an $800,000 loan backed by the SBA that allowed her to move into a larger facility in Huntington Beach.

But LuLu began to learn another lesson: too much prosperity can bring its own problems. She had a large new facility, but she couldn't move completely out of the old one in Gardena without disrupting production and losing accounts. She had to pay both mortgages for almost a year. She also purchased new equipment, increased staff, and began producing new products including frozen fruit bars.

It took her another five years to dig out of the hole that she had dug for herself by expanding too much. Finally, by the mid–1990s, things were on an even keel. For the first time, LuLu could feel she was working for herself and not for the banks from which she had borrowed heavily.

Today, you can walk into supermarkets in much of the United States, and for that matter in the United Kingdom and elsewhere around the world, and find some of the 45 products including flan, parfaits, and puddings that Lulu's Dessert Corporation sells. Her annual sales are now above $30 million. She is, by any definition of an entrepreneur, a tremendous success story.

Looking back almost 25 years, LuLu Sobrino realizes she could have made things vastly easier for herself had she only known at the beginning what she *didn't* know:

> It took me a full 10 years to learn about the legal side, the accounting side, the taxes, and the human resources of my business. Unfortunately, I usually learned from the problems I had. It was the most expensive MBA I could ever have gotten. There are so many things that can make a businessperson's life so much easier, but you have to know about them.

Her advice to a person contemplating starting a business is:

> Find your niche. Do research. Spend your money there before you put it in a business. Why? Because I hate to see businesses fail for lack of research. You have to have a business plan and that business plan has to have, on paper, all kinds of scenarios before you put money in a business. You need a prudent plan of action.

David Lizarraga, a Los Angeles–based business leader, puts it more bluntly: "I think the most important thing a businessman can address is to know what you don't know. You must know and understand all facets of your business."

While I was at the SBA, I had the great good fortune of working with the most dynamic women entrepreneur I have ever known, my deputy administrator, Melanie Sabelhaus. We meet her at length in Chapter 6.

Melanie had an outstanding marketing, sales, and management career with IBM, but left to build a hugely successful temporary executive housing company from the ground up. I turned her into a major advocate for the proposition that a new small business owner must learn what he or she doesn't know, because looking back on the growth of her own business she realized that there were aspects of her business she did not fully grasp. She then had to find and bring people on board who did. She laughingly says:

> As Hector Barreto often told me: "You have to know what you don't know." I sure had to learn. My greatest strength was selling, whether it was wigs [her first job], computers, or temporary housing. But I learned the area that I needed the greatest support in was in the financial end of my business—how to manage my business for the greatest profitability. So I learned I had to hire a great CFO, a wonderful CPA, and I had to surround myself with a quality financial advisory board who I could take my questions to and get answers even if it was a weekend or 10 o'clock at night.

Bob Lotter, an insurance and financial services marketing genius and now a technology entrepreneur and the inventor of Nice Office and the new Radar software designed to protect children from online predators, says when he started years ago, his biggest problem turned out to be lack of knowledge:

> My first challenge was a lack of capital, which is something that most new businesses experience. Then like many new entrepreneurs, I went through the challenges of lack of experience, lack of education in the field, lack of awareness of the kinds of problems I was going to have to face. I became enrolled in the School of Hard Knocks.

When I ran the Latin Business Association in Los Angeles, many members would tell us that they wanted training and information. We would spend hours and precious resources planning educational seminars, and then no one would show up. The truth is many small business owners will not dedicate the time, and sometimes money, to educate themselves. They say, "I can't spare the time away from my business." In truth, they just don't see the need. We would tell them they couldn't afford not to. If they ended up failing, as so many do within the first four years, they would have more time on their hands than they knew what to do with. I would much rather learn from experts, or others who have failed, rather than make the same mistakes myself. Education and training are the best investments you could ever make.

The example I always go back to is the one I mentioned earlier, that you must stop to sharpen your saw. Think of it as if it is your mission to cut through a thick, difficult thicket, but all you have is a dull saw to get the job done. You want to get through it as fast as possible, so you don't stop and prepare to get the job done as quickly and efficiently as possible.

That is the way many entrepreneurs approach their businesses; instead of taking the time to learn the answers that they need, they just put their head down and work as hard as they can. Typically, they don't make the progress they'd hoped for. Instead of stopping and sharpening their saw as much as possible, and then cutting through that brush in record time, they will often say they can't afford to invest that time, and learn what they need to know. I counter that they can't afford not to. It's always easier if you have the right tools to get the job done correctly. My dad would say, "If you do it right the first time, you don't have to come back and do it a second time." As usual, he was right.

The good news is it is not difficult to get the answers and assistance you need to succeed if you only stop to look. Often it's free and readily available if you're open to receiving it.

You should also commit yourself to learning as much as you can about your profession or industry throughout your career. You should read everything you can about your business. There are many resources online and professionals who offer training opportunities, sales seminars, motivational speeches, and classes that can help you improve your skills. When I attended those events, I always thought to myself, "If I can get one good idea that I can apply to my business today and improve my business, the investment of time will be more than worth it."

You should also consider volunteering your time to an organization that will contribute to your business. In my case, I have spent a great deal of time with small business organizations and chambers of commerce. When you are beginning, one of the only things of value that you can invest is your time.

Often you will not have financial resources, but you can dedicate some time to nonprofit work for the purpose of meeting prospective clients and developing strategic relationships. There's a lot to learn from others who are either in your same industry or who have been successful in their own businesses. This was a critical component to my business development activities. As I cultivated customers, I was also able to grow my business as their businesses grew. In the beginning, they needed one product or service, but as they grew and added employees, they needed additional products and services and I made sure I was able to provide them.

In the beginning, many business owners wanted to see more of a track record and told me to come back and see them in five years if I was still in business. I didn't become discouraged; I just committed myself to improving my abilities, and I was relentless in coming back every year, telling them how my business was growing, and asking for another opportunity. After a few years, the owners realized I was serious and started giving me opportunities to provide them with their insurance and financial services. Some of these businesses were very established and well-known companies in my community, and the owners of those businesses became mentors to me as well as clients.

Now, let me tell you about a small business, a construction company, started for essentially all the wrong reasons—just to make quick money—by an owner with little direct experience and, more important, an owner who did not know what he didn't know until it was too late.

The owner had very high expectations and incredible contacts. He had been successful elsewhere in a different kind of business, so he had a very positive credit history and was creditworthy. But he decided to get into a business he didn't know very well, but one that had the potential for profit. It wasn't a passion or an industry in which he had a background.

The construction business is very competitive, and if you don't know what you're doing, there are many ways it can go wrong. This owner did a lot wrong. He did not know the business well, nor did he have a good business plan or blueprint. He had a good idea and a good strategy: Go out, bid on and get big contracts, satisfy those contracts, and then move on to the next, even bigger contract.

The underlying strategy was to get in and hit a homerun as quickly as possible. There was never a sense that this was something he wanted to build for the long term or pass on to the next generation.

One of the first mistakes the owner made was that in his other, previous businesses, he never had a partner. But in this business, he needed to take on partners because he was not going to be running the day-to-day business. This, of course, was another problem. If you are not there every day, yet your name is on the business, you have a lot of exposure, especially when you're going into business with people you don't know very well. You really need to know who you're doing business with or, more important, who you are *in* business with because the worst time to find out is when you start to get into trouble.

The heart of the problem of this start-up construction company was that the owners had ambitious plans, but no contingency plans. If they didn't have instant success—didn't hit the homerun—what were they going to do? Their entire focus was on the quick hit, the instant success.

Taking on a junior partner required a division of labor. This was planned from the beginning. The owner of the business was to be the rainmaker; he would be the one to bring the business in. That was virtually his full function. The junior partner would run all the operations to fulfill the contracts, be responsible for running the office, oversee all the employees, pay the taxes, and provide other key operational duties.

This setup quickly became problematic because the owner did bring in business but he had no real idea of how the operation was running or, more important, how a construction firm should be run.

The business quickly started going south. The owner really did not have the information to make the decisions he needed to make or to have the oversight he needed to maintain. He did not even know the questions to ask. He was too dependent on somebody who, it turned out, was at least part of the problem. Yet the owner had to have complete trust in him.

One key thing this owner didn't understand was his exposure. He just assumed that because he had been successful in other businesses, he could be successful in something entirely different. He had little understanding of the true nature of the business, its risks, or its liabilities. He was in over his head, but he didn't realize it.

Sometimes you can compensate for being in over your head if your business is going well and you're making money. This provides you with a cushion to learn what you need to know as you go. But in the case of this new construction company, one of the problems they had was that in order to go after these large contracts they were acting as subcontractors, not the prime contractors; and when you operate under someone else's contract, you are fully dependent on them. What happens too often to a small company working for a large company as a subcontractor is that it does not get paid on time. The big company itself may not be paid on time but they have the resources to ride things out if their pay is late. But a small company, especially a new start-up, has no cushion. They don't have a rainy day account sitting around, so they come under pressure very quickly if they do not receive their money on time.

It's a universal problem in the construction industry. Linda Alvarado, who today owns a major general construction firm building major projects around the world, remembers her problems when she first started:

"Early on, when you start very small, the focus is on not just getting the work and getting it done, but on how am I going to get the next job? Not only do you not have enough time or capital to finish what you're doing, but the focus is always on getting more work.

"In my industry, I started as a subcontractor and getting paid quickly enough is always an issue. In construction, they hold back 10 percent, and that 10 percent is critical because that 10 percent is your profit. So cash and cash flow, early on, were very difficult for me."

The small construction company we have been examining needed many more employees than the owner was used to having and managing in his other businesses. He had been involved in family-run businesses where he had much more control over the employees and they were familiar to him. Now he had to bring in large numbers of people he really didn't know and he had not considered many of the employer-employee issues he would be facing with such a large workforce.

The owner was also traveling and leaving things up to his partner. He was, in a sense, an absentee owner. He had all of the risk and all of the liability, but he didn't have the control. Being an absentee owner in any business can be a death knell. You have to be there, paying attention to what is going on. It has to be your highest priority. It can't be a sideline, especially when there is a significant amount of money at risk. There really aren't any shortcuts. The old expression, "The harder I work, the luckier I get," is never truer than in running or growing a small business.

Things that the owner had never considered and that he really didn't know he had to worry about began to pile up for this new company, like cash flow, quarterly taxes for the large numbers of workers and employees, and the cost of operation. He simply had not realized that construction was such a capital-intensive business that required planning for the problems that arose. The new company was suddenly under crippling financial pressure not that long after they started, despite getting the kinds of contracts the owner set out to get.

The company quickly failed under the weight of a financial burden that the owner never considered when he started the enterprise.

The owner didn't know *what he didn't know* when he decided to get into a business far afield from his experience. He really needed to have done his homework before embarking on a new business venture, but he just assumed that previous successes would carry over into the new business.

Too many new businesses are started by owners who are excited by something—they know someone, or they have a contract and they figure they'll just deal with the rest of the stuff later. That's the wrong time to have to deal with your problems. Our example construction company got a big contract and—thinking that was the hard part—felt they were home free. But you have to be careful what you wish for because, instead of being the solution, that big order or big contract may just be the beginning of your problems.

Many of this new construction company's problems could have been prevented. As we see in Chapter 9, the owner could have utilized resources like the SBA, SCORE, the Small Business Development Centers or similar programs run by the states or cities, or help that is offered by many companies in the private sector. You can get technical assistance or information; you can be educated and get specific counseling from experts who have run businesses like yours; most of these options are available for free and quite a few of them are available online.

But what it all comes down to is that new business owner, regardless of the type of business, being prepared to ask for help. Sometimes business owners are too proud to seek help, but more often they simply don't realize that they need help; they don't know who to ask or what to ask. They are looking down at the problems they are facing, not up and around at what might be available to help them solve those problems. It's not their fault, they are simply too caught up in their own problem. They are reacting, instead of being proactive.

Our example construction company, the one that should have succeeded but that in the end didn't, I know a lot about this company because it was owned by my father. He had started out small, doing repairs and the like. Then he started rehabing houses and reselling them. Then he decided to go bigger, and to install tiles in apartment buildings and commercial projects. This is when he took on the partner to do the work while he went after bigger construction deals. Eventually, it got to be too much and he got out of the business, but he learned a costly lesson: Despite success in other endeavors, he could still fail if he was not very careful— and I learned this lesson from watching him.

My dad went on to be very successful in a number of different business projects. My mom was always the conservative one, and together they formed a very effective team. My mom used to ask my dad, "What will we do if you fail?" and my dad without missing a beat would say, "I'll start over and I'll build it back because I did it in the first place."

My father had unswerving confidence in himself, and that is also a key to success. You will hear many entrepreneurs I talk about in this book say they never ever considered quitting. That type of commitment is essential in being able to overcome obstacles and setbacks and in being prepared to capitalize on the next opportunity that is often just around the corner.

4

Challenge the Conventional Wisdom

Conventional wisdom is a term coined by the economist John Kenneth Galbraith in his 1958 book *The Affluent Society,* second edition (New York: Houghton & Mifflin, 1958). It is used to describe certain ideas or explanations that have become generally accepted as true. However, conventional wisdom may actually be either true or false.

Conventional wisdom often stops people in their tracks. This is not necessarily bad. If the conventional wisdom is that a small business will not survive and grow without proper financing—a truism that has been shown to be true countless times—and this rightly should act as a stumbling block to the nascent small business owner who intends to start a venture on a shoestring and hope for the best.

But conventional wisdom should not stand in the way when the belief is based on outmoded facts, wrong premises, or prejudice.

As Galbraith said, "The enemy of the conventional wisdom is not ideas, but the march of events." Take, for example, the conventional wisdom of years gone by that the construction trades are clearly a man's world and that women need not apply.

Linda Alvarado and Mercedes LaPorta have never met. They live over 2,000 miles apart, one in Denver and the other in Miami. Both are the head of successful companies they built from the ground up over many years. The stories of their phenomenal success are so identical that at first glance they seem to be the same story. Although they are not the same story, success stories of very different small businesses often seem to have the same roots.

The success of Alvarado Construction, Inc. and of Mercedes Electric Supply, Inc. have at their core the willingness of two women to follow their dreams and to challenge the conventional wisdom that neither of them had any possible chance of success. Both have found success in different facets of the construction industry, which is notably hostile to women generally. Minorities often face that same hostility in management and ownership. When both women started their businesses more than 20 years ago, women doing what they wanted to do were simply unheard of. The conventional wisdom was not simply that they would fail, but that they were crazy to even begin. However, they each pitted their will against this conventional wisdom and in the end not only succeeded beyond anyone's expectations—including quite probably their own—but, in doing so, also changed their respective industries, both for their gender and for minorities, generally.

Linda Alvarado was brought up in a highly competitive family with five brothers and no sisters. "Both my grandfathers were Protestant ministers, which was a little unusual because we are Hispanic," she remembers. "As you might imagine, our life revolved around the church."

"My parents were very, very positive people. It was clear what your priorities were growing up. There were high expectations in school that not only would you bring home an A, but you would tell them what you had learned."

Mercedes LaPorta was born in Havana, Cuba, and her family emigrated to the United States and settled in Chicago. "As I was growing up, I kind of always knew that some day I wanted to have my own business," she says. "I come from an entrepreneurial family. In Cuba, my father had his own business and my uncles had their own businesses. When we came to this country, my dad, as soon as he had saved enough money, opened up a small grocery store. I was about 13 years old, and I would work in the store on weekends. I always had this bug in me that I wanted to own my own business."

Linda Alvarado admits with a laugh she was not born an entrepreneur. "We don't have any entrepreneurial history in my family. I wasn't even a Girl Scout, so I never sold Girl Scout cookies. I never really thought about owning my own business or being my own boss."

During her college years, Linda bucked the conventional wisdom in her first work-study job. Young women worked in the cafeteria or did things like filing and answering the phone. But she took a job working for the college's landscaping department, and in doing so soon found she liked working outdoors. She began to fall in love with the construction industry. "I took very unusual classes for a woman: surveying, estimating, and construction supervision classes. This was very nontraditional as you could imagine."

After college, she went to work for a construction company. "I started actually in a project accounting position on site, later moved into a support position to a project manager, and as my skill level developed, moved into a project engineering function." In those positions, she admits, "I liked being on the construction sites as well, watching the buildings come up out of the ground. When a superstructure went up, it gave me a great sense of the creative process that ended up with this structure of great permanence and beauty."

After high school, Mercedes LaPorta went to work for the A&P supermarket chain and quickly became its first woman buyer, eventually purchasing grocery items with a budget of more than $200 million per year. She also helped end a labor strike by the chain's Mexican-dominated workforce. She could have gone on to senior management with the company, but her entrepreneurial genes surfaced about the same time she and her husband Victor decided they had enough of Chicago's winters.

Mercedes and Victor LaPorta arrived in Miami, Florida, and in March 1979 they began Mercedes Lighting, Inc. They began in a 1,000-square-foot office selling only Sylvania light bulbs. The decision to start her own business was simple. She says, "I always had this bug in me that I wanted to own my own business. I really never wanted to work for anybody else, my first job in Chicago was one born of necessity."

Just three years before Mercedes and Victor LaPorta arrived in Miami, Linda Alvarado had decided to get into the construction business by starting small:

> As I was on these construction sites, there were very, very large projects going on. I began to dream about building a project of my own. It was a pretty modest dream at the time and I began to think of it as a possibility. I decided I would start a small construction management company.
>
> My start was very nontraditional. Many times, you draw up a business plan and follow it. I never dreamed of owning a business. I started very, very small, working in the development.
>
> Of course, banks didn't like to fund construction companies. To make a long story short, I had this blue suit and I went to several banks, but I was rejected by all of them, six banks. My parents finally mortgaged their house for me to get going for $2,500. It was the bridge money needed to get me over the gap until I was able to get a small business loan. Perseverance and persistence have kept me going. They are very important to the extent that I believe I will outwork most people in finding a solution.
>
> This led to starting a company as a curb cutter and doing sidewalks and foundation work—it was really a foundation for building my business to what it is today.

The growth of both the companies started by these two women has been nothing short of inspirational.

Less than 10 years after it started, Mercedes Electric had achieved its goal of being one of the leaders in the distribution of electrical equipment in South Florida. By 1992, the company became Mercedes Electric Supply, Inc. and moved into a 30,000-square-foot warehouse and office building, housing over $2 million worth of inventory.

The company Mercedes now heads acts as an electrical, automation, and data communications distributor that employs 45 workers, has annual sales of over $25 million, and is growing rapidly. It ranks among the 200 largest electrical supply houses in the country. In the past couple of years, as Miami International Airport has undergone a significant expansion and rehabilitation, Mercedes Electric Supply, Inc. has won the largest contracts in its history. First, it won a $10.2 million contract from American Airlines to supply the electric distribution and lighting system for its new terminal. Then it won a $9.2 million subcontract from the general contractor doing the South Terminal modernization and now has started a $3 million contract on the North Terminal modernization.

Linda Alvarado never lost her dream of building grand projects. Her small sidewalk and foundation company morphed into a small general construction firm and soon became one of the fastest growing commercial general contracting firms in the country. It was one of three firms that built the new Denver Broncos stadium and was also part of the construction of the Denver International Airport and the Colorado Convention Center. Today, it employs 450 workers and has revenues in the multimillions, building projects for public and private sectors, both domestically and internationally.

Both Linda Alvarado and Mercedes LaPorta are successful not because they had some better idea for a new product or service. Both, after all, are in very settled, old line industries. Although both brought innovative techniques to what they do, so did their competitors. Nor are they successful simply because they worked hard. When talking about their years in the construction industry, their stories of what they overcame are so similar that you realize they succeeded because they stood up to decades of prejudice. They chose not just to ignore the conventional wisdom, but to meet it head-on and steamroll right over it.

Their stories of their early years are very alike. Mercedes remembers with a laugh:

> It's hard enough for a woman to start a new small business, but it's doubly hard when that business is typically a "man's business." When I started 28 years ago, I don't remember running into a woman anywhere in this industry down here in South Florida. I had a lot of doors slammed in my face. In the early years, I had to use whatever tools might be available to me to break in. In those times, I was kind of relegated to the back room because I couldn't get my foot in the door anywhere. So my partner, who was a man, would have to go out to make all the calls.

Linda remembers that, at that time, women just weren't welcomed on construction sites:

> I experienced graffiti being written on the walls and pictures of me in various stages of undress. Nevertheless, I worked with some really good people and I knew this was an industry that I really wanted to stay a part of.

Being optimistic by nature gave me some sense of personal mission to show that women could succeed in this field. You have to smile because what people are looking for when I walk in the room is somebody six foot five and burley. And in reality, I'm five foot five.

I would be asked, "Do you know what you're doing . . . Do you know you're not going to be welcome?" I was never directly told I couldn't do it, but it was indirect. I was once told, "You have so much potential, have you looked at other fields like teaching or corporate America or even law school?" At the time, women were just making their initial inroads in those fields. "Why don't you look at areas you could fit in?" I was told. I overheard conversations and jokes about me from many people. It was an environment where being the first led to guys putting an arm around me and saying, "What's a nice girl like you doing in a place like this?"

But instead of becoming discouraged, the hostility made both women dig in their heels and try that much harder.

Mercedes says:

But, in all these 28 years, I've never considered there was anything I wouldn't be able to overcome, whatever problems I had at the time. I always knew I would find a way to do it, and I always did find a way to overcome the obstacles that were in my way.

When a person told me I was going to fail, I just looked him or her straight in the eye and said it would never happen.

Linda remembers:

It was for me, at the same time, both hurtful and challenging. When your credibility is questioned, it's very easy to personalize the criticism, and I had to be very careful not to disqualify myself from opportunities, not to believe the conventional thinking, and not to put myself into a box. That was my biggest challenge. While no one ever told me I would fail, I'm sure there were some bets I would.

My mother always told me you have to start small but think big. That was reinforcement to me and reminds me today that all businesses started as small businesses. Without some pain, there can never be gain. The key is balancing that and measuring that. That little sentence let me go back and rethink and, if nothing else, say, "Look, I'm no different than anyone else in a pickup with a briefcase."

Both have now gone on to be so much more than just business successes.

Mercedes LaPorta is active in numerous civic and business groups including the Women's Business Enterprise National

Council (WBENC), Women President's Organization, the National Minority Supplier Development Corporation, National Electrical Contractors Association, and the National Association of Women in Construction. She is a passionate advocate for women in business, serves on the Enterprising Woman National Advisory Board, and is a WBENC ambassador who works to get large corporations to recognize the importance of supporting the growth of women-owned businesses. She has become a mentor especially to women starting out who own their own businesses.

In the mid-1980s, Linda Alvarado started a company called Palo Alto Inc., with her husband Robert. Palo Alto built and now runs more than 100 fast-food restaurants, including Taco Bell, Pizza Hut, and Kentucky Fried Chicken locations.

In the early 1990s, she heard that the Colorado Rockies baseball franchise was up for sale. "I had never considered owning a professional sports team," Alvarado says. But the more she thought about it, the more she liked the idea. No woman had ever tried to buy a Major League Baseball franchise. "It was a huge risk for a woman, especially a Hispanic woman, to own a sports team." But at age 39, she became part owner of the Colorado Rockies.

She now is a corporate director for three Fortune 150 companies and has served as the chairman of the board of the Denver Hispanic Chamber of Commerce and as a commissioner of the White House Initiative for Hispanic Excellence in Education.

But every day both of them still worry about their businesses. Mercedes confides:

> Right now, my business is getting ready to make another significant step in size and volume. So I'm preparing myself for this next step forward by adding technology tools. We have had computer systems and technology for a long time, but as we grow we will need more and more to service our growing customer base. In my warehouse, I'm now using automated handheld devices that will print out orders and inventory. Everything is done by bar codes so that the filling of orders is more accurate and quicker and deliveries can be scheduled automatically. This eliminates errors, it saves us time and money, and above all it upgrades our level of customer service. If we make it easier for our customers, we make it easier for ourselves.

Linda Alvarado admits:

> I worry about cash flow, labor, backlogs, cost of insurance, and all sorts of other things. But when I get up in the morning, I can't be paranoid that people are after me.
>
> People measure success very differently. My success has come from my ability to enable others—the people who work for me and with me—and to understand that change is constant. In order to be at the top of your game, you have to be able to adapt to change. The only reason I'm a success is I empower those around me to meet our clients' expectations and to make them understand that it's part of their dream also.

Starting off in a man's world, what central lesson have these remarkable women learned on their way to success beyond not paying attention to the common wisdom?

"There are ways to play the game within the rules, but still find ways to win," says Linda Alvarado.

"I think it was the way I was raised, my father raised me always telling me that if you set your mind to do something then there's nothing you can't do," says Mercedes LaPorta. "If you put everything you have into it, you're going to succeed.

"And I've always carried that with me. My dad passed away a few years ago, but all my life he was my inspiration."

Before women like Linda Alvarado and Mercedes LaPorta bucked the odds to achieve success, the conventional wisdom held that women have no place in the construction trades. Likewise, the conventional wisdom has held that certain things are done a certain way and only a certain way. Take, for instance, how office supplies used to be sold.

It all started with a broken printer ribbon on a Fourth of July weekend in 1985. Tom Stemberg, who had recently lost his job as a supermarket chain marketing executive, was trying to print a business plan for an entrepreneurial venture he was considering when his printer ribbon broke. The local stationery store, where Tom bought his office supplies, was closed for the holiday. As he drove from store to store without finding the ribbon he needed, he grew more and more annoyed. But at the same time, he came to realize that there was something basically wrong with the way

office supplies were being sold. He became a man with a mission,
and 10 months later, the first supermarket for office products was
open for business. Staples, the Office Superstore, was born and
today has 1,900 stores around the world and does $15 billion in
annual volume.

But before that first store was a success, the conventional wisdom on how office products are sold had to be reinvented. Tom
told me:

> When we started out, the biggest difference in our concept was that we
> were half price, and in some cases even more. For instance, the same case
> of copy paper that the little stationery store in Washington, DC, or Kansas
> City, Missouri, was selling for $65 or $70, we sold for $25. The ballpoint
> pens that might be selling for $3.25 each elsewhere—and if you were
> smart you might be able to work a 10 percent discount—we sold for
> 89 cents.
>
> The other major difference was we really sold everything. In those
> days, if you wanted an office machine, you went to an office machine
> dealer; a computer, you went to a computer store; software you got from
> a software store. You went to a janitorial supply store to get janitorial sup-
> plies and to an office supply store to get office supplies. That sounds
> strange today, but that's the way it was.
>
> Staples has all that under one roof and at half price. While the typical
> office supply store might be open from nine to five, Monday through
> Friday, Staples was open 7:00 AM to 9:00 PM six days a week, and soon
> after on Sundays, too. We had a complete stock, at half price, and had
> convenient hours.

This just wasn't the way things were done and this presented
Stemberg with a pair of related problems. First, he had to convince
shoppers to come to his store for all their needs. Then, even more
critical, he had to get suppliers, especially makers of brand
name goods, to sell to him. They just didn't get his concept; most
thought he would likely go broke, but worse, if he succeeded, they
knew, given his business model of discounting, prices would end
up being cut across the board, and they stood to have to lower
wholesale prices, which would drive their profit margins down.

He believed in the concept, but if he couldn't get suppliers to
buy in, he wouldn't be able to offer consumers the kinds of choices
that were central to his concept.

Some reluctant suppliers he convinced by showing them that they would actually profit more from the volume he was going to do, even if the margin dropped a bit. What he did was go to the suppliers and tell them that his business model was going to work and it was the wave of the future. He likened it to a train and told them it was time for them to, as he put it, "Get on board or get run over."

Others, he simply took by the hand and showed them the future:

> One way we turned around reluctant suppliers was by taking their people through one of our stores. I remember Canon, who made the hottest business machine back in those days, the Canon PC6 copier. Canon would not sell them to us. I got the Canon sales manager to come to our store at noontime on a Wednesday and when he saw the mob of people shopping there he said, "No problem, I'll open your account immediately."

Little by little, the suppliers bought into his concept. In the end, those players ended up doing very well because, as he had promised, while their margins may have been smaller, the volume of business was such that their profits actually increased.

The conventional wisdom of retailing was you couldn't do it the way Tom Stemberg was proposing, but he had the nerve to go it on his own. He quickly revolutionized an industry.

While the notion seems quaint these days, it has not been that long ago that the conventional wisdom was that a "women's place is in the home." We have already met Linda Alvarado and Mercedes LaPorta and throughout this book, we meet other women who founded businesses and then developed them into not just successes, but in many cases into international powerhouses that occupy important places in our economy.

I have long been an advocate of encouraging women to take the leap and listen to the entrepreneurial spirits inside them. While I was at the SBA, my deputy Melanie Sabelhaus took the lead in developing new and innovative ways to help women overcome the stereotype and conventional thinking that women don't start up businesses.

In Chapter 6, we hear the full story of Rebecca Matthias, a woman who started out selling maternity clothes to a few friends and who today is the world's largest manufacturer and retailer of maternity clothing and runs some 1,500 retail stores. She, like Melanie, is a passionate advocate for the idea that the conventional wisdom is wrong and a women's place is in starting enterprises of all sorts. Rebecca says:

> I'm a huge advocate of women starting businesses, and I think every woman should start a business. I believe every woman has the capability. I speak on this subject often, and at some point I look out into the audience and tell the women there: "You could start and grow a great business." Sometimes they look at me and say, "Nobody ever said that to me."
>
> It's not offered as a major at any college or university—starting up a small business. So women don't think of it when they think about their careers or what they're going to do with their lives. I really didn't think that either when I started out. My training was as an architect and in construction engineering and that was going to be my career. That was my first job, and I never thought about starting a business. But obviously, somewhere in the back of my mind, I must've been thinking about it. Then I became pregnant with my first child and that's when I really began thinking about starting a business. I think that's when a lot of women start thinking about it because they have to try to put together work and family and there's not many ways to go about it. There's not a lot of flexibility in either job, but you do have some when you start a business.
>
> I think that's one thing that motivates a lot of women, and I wish that women would take it to the next step and start a business. In my case, I had a lot of support and encouragement to do that because my husband is very entrepreneurial and so was my family. My father started businesses a couple of times and even though he was not all that successful, he was supportive. I think that's something that people really need to have in their lives if they're going to successfully start businesses. They need support and encouragement because business doesn't go in a straight line. It's not a formula and you have your ups and downs, but you have to keep at it.
>
> I think that business ownership by women is the next evolutionary step, the next step in the revolution that began back in the 1970s. All of a sudden, women started going into the workplace. It's hard for kids today to even understand, but when I was growing up, most women didn't even attempt to have any kind of professional life, especially after the children were born. They were teachers, secretaries, and nurses; and thank goodness they were teachers because of the energy they poured into teaching. It was more than a glass ceiling; it was a self-imposed limitation. They focused on family, which of course is not a bad thing, but then things changed. Women were not satisfied with that, and we had a real revolution starting in the 1970s.

Women were going to law school and entering professions and I think it was harder than anybody thought it was going to be—having two jobs. I haven't seen many men step up to the challenge of raising the kids while having a career. This seems still to be falling mainly in the laps of women. When you try to balance a family with a career, it's hard—it's really hard. I think it's obvious that the answer is to start your own business. You certainly don't work less but you have the flexibility. You work when you want to and you can change your lifestyle. You can start small and get big later. You can put things on a hiatus and go back to them. You're in control. And it just seems like the obvious move for women to make who have ambitions at the same time that they have motherhood. It's just a great solution, and I don't think we've found many other solutions for combining work and motherhood. It's natural that we move into this next step and I think we're going to see more women starting their own businesses because they are capable of it and the reward is so huge, not just financially, but in personal satisfaction.

Conventional wisdom can take many forms. When someone comes along to challenge it, his or her success can teach valuable lessons. Take, for instance, the inspiring success story of David Lizarraga.

David, who is an old and close friend, grew up in the East Los Angeles barrio. He was a young social activist, and in 1973 he became president of the East Los Angeles Community Union—known by its acronym TELACU—a nonprofit community development corporation founded in 1968.

Shortly after taking over the organization, TELACU received a federal grant of $10 million that David characterized as, "a lot of money, but not enough to create a whole lot of change when there's millions and millions of dollars in need."

Typically—you might call it the conventional wisdom—when organizations get government grants, they run various kinds of training programs or try to restart enterprises; and when the grant money runs out, they go hat in hand back to the government for additional grants to do it all over again. David realized he had to break that hand-to-mouth cycle and change the conventional way grant money was spent. So he turned TELACU into a kind of nonprofit holding company controlling a series of for-profit companies that benefited the community through thousands of jobs and whose profits have now funded more than three decades of social programs.

"I never started out as a businessman," David remembers. "I was a community organizer so the idea of starting a business that would create businesses in East Los Angeles was kind of foreign to me. But our community was so disinvested when companies moved out. So starting a business was a way to bring reinvestment back into the community."

One of David's first decisions was to use grant money so that TELACU could buy 50 acres of land—the site of an old factory that had closed and laid off 2,000 workers—and convert it into an industrial park. Then he put on his salesman's hat and went out to find investors so that businesses could be started in the park.

It was a tough sell, but gradually David succeeded and the TELACU Development Corporation was born. Businesses were started and workers from the community were hired. "We believed in tough love," he says. "We gave a job to anyone who needed it, but we said 'You gotta show up, five days a week, and if you don't, there's plenty others that will.'" Today, the industrial park employs over 3,000 people.

The early days were not easy. "At the beginning of TELACU, there was lack of planning," David remembers. "The organization started more as a concept than anything else. It was a nonprofit organization whose purpose was to put together for-profit businesses. That was a very unique model that actually is no longer allowed. The organization still exists as a nonprofit holding company of for-profit subsidiaries, but we learned from trial and error."

After the development company was started, TELACU entered the financial services sector, opening the first branch of the Community Commerce Bank in 1976. David says, "For Latinos to grow, they needed access to capital, but that just wasn't there. Banks were unresponsive." Today, TELACU has $200 million in assets with eight lending institutions in underserved communities. Latinos account for 80 percent of loans and delinquency has been low, leading many traditional banks to reenter the inner-city market they had once shunned. "We are good risks," David says of Latinos.

The organization now controls TELACU Industries, TELACU Residential Management, TELACU Real Estate Services, South Coast Shingle Company (one of Southern California's most established building materials supply companies), the Tamayo Restaurant, TELACU Construction and its subsidiary Pyramid Plumbing, TELACU Construction Management, and Inter-City Energy Systems.

TELACU has for a long time not had to rely on new grants. Because of its for-profit holding company, TELACU Industries, the organization is now completely self-sustaining. It has assets of close to $500 million and annual revenue of $120 million, and has quickly moved into the ranks of the top 100 businesses in Los Angeles. Eighty percent of profits are directed into TELACU-owned interests, including real estate, lending, and small- and medium-sized businesses, while 20 percent goes toward community social programs such as educational resource centers, training programs, and its renowned LINC TELACU Education Foundation (LTEF) that provides college scholarships for hundreds of students every year.

David Lizzaraga was a community activist who became an entrepreneur out of necessity. The conventional wisdom was that an activist bucks the system. In David's case, he ignored that conventional wisdom and not only embraced the system but also made it work for him and for his community.

There is a lesson in that for us all.

5

No Guts, No Glory

FEAR NOT MISTAKES

Another piece of conventional wisdom is "Always learn from your mistakes." This, I can tell you from my own personal experience as well as from talking with those who have made it big, is conventional wisdom that is definitely true.

Earlier, I related the story of my father's construction company's failure, which occurred mainly because, at the time, he did not realize it was fundamentally different from the other successful businesses he was running. I attribute the failure to not knowing what he did not know. I learned much from this episode, and perhaps the most important lesson for me was that failure does not have to be permanent.

For some, a huge mistake forces them to doubt themselves and to abandon ship. It's not about what happens, but what you do about it. Not succeeding in business is not necessarily a failure if you learn from the mistake. There are countless examples of very

66

successful entrepreneurs who failed more than once before they became the successes they are today. We have met and will meet more than one in these pages.

Throughout this book, we hear the same message from many of the most successful entrepreneurs: Learn from your mistakes. One thing they have in common is they were able, just as my father was, to learn from their mistakes. Some even go so far as to say they succeeded later because they had failed and were able to learn from that failure.

Fred Ruiz built his frozen food empire over the years by meeting challenges as they arose, and he admits to making more than his fair share of mistakes:

> Over my business career, I can't pinpoint any one single big mistake, but I sure can pinpoint many small mistakes that I made. The important thing always is to learn from those mistakes, to learn from each and every one of those mistakes so that you do not make that same mistake again. That is the important issue. There can be a silver lining in every mistake you make. I don't care what the issue is in business, or in life generally, there's always something positive you can learn from every mistake that will help you be a better person or a better businessperson. I have my 10,000 mistakes, but we're a better company from having learned from those 10,000 mistakes.
>
> Learning from every mistake is really important. Many times people underestimate the commitment and the amount of work that's required to build a successful business. And I also think that people underestimate the time line that it takes and believe that they only have to work hard for a few years and then it will be a gravy train. I think people starting out in business are often overly optimistic about the amount of time and money it takes to build a successful business.

Linda Alvarado, who built her construction company into an international giant, has an interesting view of mistakes:

> The biggest mistake I made early on was thinking I couldn't make mistakes. That was a mistake. Perhaps the desire to succeed and excel makes you fear mistakes. Risk taking is what allows us to move forward, but it has to be balanced and measured. We're not always perfect in what we do. We all need to learn and sometimes you learn from your mistakes.
>
> One thing I didn't do at the start was go back when I didn't win the work to ask why I hadn't won. Losing was so painful, and it is challenging

to go back and ask for a debriefing. I could have heard they were worried
about my lack of a track record or my lack of capital, but it would have
given me the opportunity to have face time with that potential client and,
more importantly, to thank them for the opportunity to bid on the job
and to ask for another opportunity. The ability to do this is something, I
think, that evolves over time. The natural inclination when you don't get a
job is simply to walk away and to move on to something else. The feedback you get when you lose is sometimes even more valuable than
celebrating when you get a job or get a contract. It's looking at the
companies who didn't make it and asking why, more than looking at
the companies who did make it.

Al Frink—who we met earlier and who until recently was
assistant secretary for Manufacturing and Services in the
International Trade Administration of the U.S. Department of
Commerce—built his internationally recognized carpet manufacturing company, Fabrica International, from the ground up.
He says he made more than his fair share of mistakes: "Every mistake I've ever made I've learned from. I can't think of many
mistakes I would take off the table because the lessons I learned
from them were so valuable. It was a learning experience that
always helped with the next step. So even if I go back and look
and say I could have done this thing or that differently, I think I
wouldn't because of the lessons I learned from doing it wrong.
Mistakes help create future good decisions. No one could make
every decision without error. But the beauty of those mistakes is
how you take the knowledge you learn from the mistakes and
apply it to your next decision."

Trailblazers don't usually fear making a mistake.

BE WILLING TO RISK

"No risk, no reward" is certainly a piece of conventional wisdom
that is almost universally embraced by entrepreneurs who have
made it. Many owners can trace the development of their companies, in fact the development of themselves as entrepreneurs, to a
point where they had to take what at the time seemed to be a huge
personal or business risk, and the fact that they took the risk and
survived is what has propelled them along the path to success.

Al Frink started out as many young people did in his day—delivering newspapers and selling subscriptions. He says it taught him a lot, lessons that eventually stood him in good stead as he built his business:

> Do not be afraid of taking risks. Being risk adverse is not going to lead to success. Many things in life are risks, everything you do is a risk. Don't be afraid to fail. Look at the people around you who have succeeded and don't assume that they were simply lucky. They put their abilities into the marketplace and took risks. Many times they were willing to reach out and risk failure in order to succeed.
>
> Going door-to-door trying to sell newspaper subscriptions, I often got those doors slammed in my face. But it taught me to deal with rejection, and on a certain level to deal with failure so that when I got to the point in my life where I was risk taking, I was not afraid to take a risk.
>
> At one point in my life, success scared me because I didn't have a lot of experience with success. But failure didn't scare me because I had a lot of experience with failure. This experience with failure allowed me to take risks because I was not afraid. And it stuck with me today because I'm still very much a risk taker.

Most teenagers are looking forward perhaps to a first car—used, of course—but Harold Doley knew at age 13 what he wanted—to own a seat on the New York Stock Exchange. When he finally had enough money, he went for it, but it was a tremendous risk for a young African American to take. Doley says:

> You have to believe in yourself. I'm a risk taker. Everyone said I shouldn't be doing what I'm doing. When I was younger, I was something of a gunslinger. I would take risks on trades. For many years, I was a "name" at Lloyd's of London. Lloyd's imploded in the mid-1990s, but because I had been trained as an accountant, when I looked at a financial statement, I understood the fundamentals of investing so I could calculate the risk and I did not take losses.
>
> There is an old story that one day J. P. Morgan was walking down the street and a person came up to him and said, "Mr. Morgan I'm an investor in a company I know you are involved in and I'm so worried I can't sleep at night. What should I do?" Morgan said, "Sell until you reach the point you can sleep at night."
>
> You have to feel secure in your risk. Life is full of risk. If you want to succeed, if you want to do things, you're going to have to first believe in yourself; you have to ignore what people say trying to discourage you

from reaching your goals. The basic approach is setting goals and trying to achieve them on a daily basis.

Mercedes LaPorta counsels many young entrepreneurs, especially young women, who want to emulate her success. She at times has risked everything to make her electrical supply business one of the biggest in the Southeast. So she knows what the stakes in starting a small business can be. She says:

> Whenever I meet a young person who wants to start their own business, the first thing I asked them is: "Are you a risk taker? Are you willing to risk everything you have? If that moment comes when you have to put everything you have on the line, will you be ready?"
>
> In the 28 years I've been in business, I've had to put my home, everything I had, including my kid's future, on the dotted line. I had to be ready to possibly lose it all. On more than one occasion, in order to get the financing I needed to allow my business to survive, I had to put everything I owned on the line; to put my entire net worth back into the business. If you're not willing to do that, take those kinds of risks, then go work for somebody else because there's going to come that time in your business when you're going to need to make those kinds of decisions, going to need to take that kind of risk, if you're in it for the long haul.

But, of course, there are times when risk flows over into foolhardiness. There are risks that are simply too big to take. So taking risk must always be tempered by finding ways to manage that risk.

For Al Frink, the answer is to start out slow and build up gradually. He says, "Never underestimate your own ability to succeed. Never underestimate your own potential. Study those who have failed so you can learn from their failures. But only take little risks at first, so you're able to build your confidence. It's simply taking small steps before you take the big ones."

Meet Bob Lorsch, one of the most successful serial entrepreneurs I know. He has succeeded spectacularly, and failed just as spectacularly. This has given him a most interesting take on mistakes, risk, on instinct, and the interaction between them. Bob says:

> I've been in business now for 38 years. Another way to look at that is I've been making mistakes—some big, some small but hopefully not too many big—for all those years. But what's important, what's critical, is to learn every time you make a mistake so you don't repeat the same mistake.

I don't think about my mistakes very often. The thing about life, and about business, is that you get re-dos. You don't have to be right every time. You can be successful being right 51 percent of the time. You never stop making mistakes. If you stop making mistakes, you stop being human. But the smart thing is to make fewer of them or to recognize them sooner. To an extent, mistakes are almost good because you learn things, and without that knowledge you can't really be successful.

This brings us to risk and to Lorsch's unusual take on how to face risk. The bottom line, he says, is simply to trust your own instincts:

Without mistakes, you can't learn; if you don't learn, you can't be successful. If you're stuck with safety and security and no mistakes, and you resist change, you can't really be successful. Without risk, without taking chances, you will never succeed.

It is unusual to be able to have reward without risk. You have to take risks, but the question is how you reduce risk to a manageable level. I've found I do it by trusting my own instincts.

In school, the teacher always told you that when you were taking a multiple-choice test, the chances were the first answer you came up with was the right one. If you went back and second-guessed yourself and changed that answer, more often than not, you would be changing it to an incorrect one.

Lorsch says for him, life and business are very much like that multiple-choice test: The first answer he comes up with is, more likely than not, the correct one:

The brain is a very unique kind of computer. When you make mistakes, it feels pain, disappointment, frustration, and loss. It programs those things into its databank. Hopefully, it prepares you with the tools and the instincts so you don't make those same mistakes again. If you do, it's really your fault. I've made a lot of mistakes, but given where I'm sitting today, I think I have been right at least 51 percent of the time. All the mistakes have given me the tools to be right more times than not.

Over the years, I have been constantly processing mistakes and success. When I am faced with taking a risk, I don't sit down and plot it all out on a spreadsheet. If it feels right, I go for it. I've found that 9 out of 10 times it was right. I just do it based on personal experience. I meet challenges from an instinctive level. My experience gives me the tools to be right most times. Now I find if I am about to make a mistake, I just pull back and that is based on experience and usually I am able to correct on the fly.

Obviously, Lorsch is able to evaluate risk and manage it based on almost four decades of experience. There are few situations he encounters that don't fall into a "been-there-done-that" scenario. But what about the person just starting out in business—someone who does not have the lifetime of experience that Bob Lorsch has?

"When you're young, you don't have the experience," he admits. "But there are plenty of people you can find who do. Seek them out. I know I'm always happy to help with some advice and I'm sure most successful businessmen are also.

Some degree of risk is reasonable and acceptable. Sometimes even greater risk is still manageable. But, as I said, then there is a degree of risk that borders on or even crosses over into foolhardiness. Consider, if you will, a now famous story concerning FedEx founder Fred Smith back in FedEx's very early days.

As with Staples and its founder Tom Stemberg, it's hard to think of an international giant like FedEx as anything but the ubiquitous worldwide delivery organization with trucks in every city and a fleet of planes second in size in the world only to American Airlines.

But it was far from that once. It was born, so to speak, in 1966 in a Yale University senior term paper for Professor Challis A. Hall Jr.'s Economics 43A class. Written by young Frederick Smith, the paper outlined an imaginary national air delivery service that relied on a "hub and spoke" system in which all packages were brought to a central location, sorted, and then sent back out for delivery. This was true even of packages going from point to point in the same city.

Regretfully, Professor Hall died in 1968 and never lived to see what the idea became. He gave young Fred Smith a "gentlemen's C" noting the paper was well constructed and well written, but the central concept would never work.

Fred Smith graduated and went on to Vietnam as a marine lieutenant, was discharged in 1969, and got married. He was from a moderately wealthy family—his father at one time owned the Toddle House restaurant chain, and he used some family money when he returned to the United States to purchase a troubled aircraft sales business, Arkansas Aviation Sales, Inc. At age 25, he bought the ailing business, and moved his new wife to Little Rock, Arkansas.

Under the guidance of the budding entrepreneur, the business did better, earning $250,000 in its second year on sales of about $9 million.

In 1970, he found he could buy French-made Falcon 20 jets from Pan American World Airlines, their U.S. representatives, at well under the plane's market value. This was at a time when aircraft sales, especially new aircraft, were in a depressed state, and Pan American had taken possession of too large an inventory of the small, fast planes.

As he had been in college, Smith was still fascinated by the air cargo industry and determined to get into the business because he saw the commercial airlines doing such a poor job of it. So he hatched a plan to buy several of Pan American's Falcons, take out the seats, and replace the door with a wider door he would have to invent, and fly them as cargo aircraft.

His business idea slowly evolved and he was up to his eyeballs in debt and was almost out of working capital. Truthfully, the fledgling company was poised on a precipice. Smith had taken risk after risk and now, unless he could get sizable permanent financing, it was about to go bust.

He now turned to Chicago industrialist Henry Crown. Smith met with Crown and tried to convince him that bailing Federal Express out was a good decision because its Falcons, and the option it held to buy more, was worth more than the money he was asking for.

Various meetings ensued and various financing plans sprung up including ones that had Smith giving up 80 percent of his stock in the company, but things stalled for various complex reasons. Smith was pretty much tapped out as he left Chicago one Friday night, headed back to Arkansas, and didn't know how he would meet payroll and pay his fuel bill on Monday morning. Here a legend was born about an entrepreneur who was willing to take a risk well beyond the manageable in an effort to save his company.

Fred Smith has only once told this story, which has now grown to almost mythic proportions. But some of those at the company with him at that time confirm it actually did happen.

Smith got to the Chicago airport and saw there was a flight to Las Vegas at the gate next to his. He cashed in his ticket and bought one to the gambling capital. Over the weekend, he took the few hundred in cash he had left and turned it into almost $30,000—enough to meet the payroll and pay for the aviation fuel he needed for the next week.

His employees in Memphis remember that he called on Friday night, depressed he had not worked out his deal with Crown, and told them that on Monday they might or might not have a company. Then he came in on Monday with just enough cash to get by and only later told them how he had acquired it.

Smith said he might have been able to keep the doors open another week, but he considered what happened an omen of better things to come. It was. He was able to consummate a deal with Crown and General Dynamics, then other investors came forward, and, as they like to say, the rest is history.

Fred Smith was a man with a dream and with an absolute certitude that he could overcome any risk almost by force of will. He did not so much manage risk as ignore it. Many other small business owners have done the same with disastrous consequences. In the end, Smith might be a better example of what happens when the degree of risk becomes unacceptable—or he might be the prime example of how force of will can make any degree of risk acceptable if not manageable.

Is there any way to gauge your maximum level of risk? SCORE counselor Bob d'Augustino has a method when he is advising potential new businesses owners. He says:

> The way I ask them to manage risk is by asking what would happen if they were unable to pay this 19 percent loan? Would they lose their house, condominium, or co-op? What would it mean to the family? Would their son or daughter have to come home from college?
>
> I tell them if the risk goes beyond the point that you're not willing to pay, then you should wait. If they tell me that they're willing to take that level of risk, fine. If they say no, they're not willing to do that, or they're not willing to get a co-signer, then I advise them to wait. If a wife is not willing to co-sign the loan, I'll usually bring her in at that stage and ask, "Are you comfortable with the risk your husband is willing to take?"
>
> And if she says no, then I will tell them I think they're wrong. We at SCORE cannot order a couple to do something, but we tell them that

there's a risk that we don't think they should take. They should wait a while, become better prepared, and then come back and we'll see what we can do. So we cannot decide what level of risk is comfortable for them.

Some fellows say I'm willing to take that risk, the family says we're willing to take that risk, then I say, "Okay, you're going in with open eyes, you know something can happen, and as long as you recognize that, fine. I don't want you to be surprised." The worst thing in a small business is to be surprised because in 40 years that I've been in business I've never been surprised when it was good news. It's always bad news—I forgot to do something or I did something wrong—and it usually costs me money or costs me a client; so we try to minimize surprises. If they go in with their eyes open, then I'm comfortable.

Bob McKinley is the regional director and associate vice president for economic development of the University of Texas, San Antonio's Institute for Economic Development. We meet him at greater length in Chapter 9. Bob has had a long career dealing with small business, and he has an interesting view on today's new small business person's willingness to take risk.

"I believe people starting small businesses today are less risk adverse because the culture of the corporate parent is really not dominant." he told me. "We're getting to three generations away from the Depression-era, so I don't think we have that same reference point. The last generations have grown up in the more affluent situation and, generally speaking, the country's been on a roll."

EMBRACE CHANGE

If you are to succeed as a small business person, you have to be willing to take risks and find ways to manage that risk. But just as risk is part of owning a business, so is change. You have to accept the fact that almost inevitably as your business grows it will change and often change in ways you might never have anticipated. If your business is to survive and grow, you must expect that change is a part of the process, and you must welcome change and embrace it.

Management guru Peter F. Drucker said, "The entrepreneur always searches for change, responds to it, and exploits it as an opportunity."

Don't be complacent; business will keep changing. It must keep changing, or eventually it will become obsolete, and will have no reason to exist. Jim Collins, in his book *Good to Great: Why Some Companies Make the Leap and Others Don't* (New York: HarperCollins, 2001) describes many major corporations that have become extinct. In recent history, we have the examples of Enron, Arthur Andersen, WorldCom, and others.

Larry Bossidy and Ram Charan, in *Confronting Reality: Doing What Matters to Get Things Right* (New York: Crown, 2004), talk about the concept of being able to look around the corner. That is really good advice, and it is something that must be practiced. A CEO of a major technology company once said, "That I'm paranoid, doesn't mean they're not out to get me." He was talking about the competition. We know that competition is good and forces us to change. In the end, it makes us better, so we should not be afraid of it. We should welcome change and take advantage of the opportunities that are presented because of it.

One of the best stories I heard that captured this concept for me is the story Earl Graves, the founder of *Black Enterprise* magazine told me when I visited him in his New York office some years ago.

He was an aide for Robert Kennedy and was with him during his presidential contest in the early 1960s. He told me that he was completely committed to working for Kennedy and was part of his team when Kennedy was assassinated. After that, Earl says he didn't know what to do. The only thing he could think of was starting a business from an idea that he had.

He wanted to start a magazine for the African American business community. He told me that he went to every bank he could in New York to get the financing for his small business. However, nobody believed that he could be a success. He wasn't sure if he would ever get the business going. Finally, a banker told him he would give him his loan. He told Earl that he didn't believe that he would make it, but because it was a SBA guaranteed loan, the government would pay him back most of his money when the business failed.

Earl Graves was a proud man, but this was his chance. He accepted that loan and worked very hard to make *Black Enterprise* magazine a success. He remembers that one of his most satisfying experiences was paying back that loan early and in full, proving to that banker that he really did know what he was talking about.

Earl has gone on to have an incredibly successful business career, starting new businesses, like one of the largest soft drink bottling corporations on the East Coast, and serving on a number of Fortune 500 boards of directors. In the meantime, he has also assisted and helped countless small businesses in the African American community through the magazine and the organizations he contributes to. Earl Graves is a success by any measure, but he is also someone truly welcomed and embraced change and made the most of it.

Harold Doley has become one of America's most successful security broker-dealers. "You have to understand and recognize your market," he says. "You have to be nimble enough to adapt to your marketplace. That is critical. You have to be able to adapt. You have to be focused, but you have to understand that life is full of vicissitudes and full of change. The old saying that the only thing that's constant in life is change is true. You have to recognize that. I'm in a business where you get hit, but the important thing is you have to get up, and keep going. You are going to have your successes, but you're also going to have your reversals. You diversify, and you keep moving.

"You have to be able to expand. You might start out in business with an African American base, but then you have to bring in Hispanic customers and from there you have to go more broadly to an urban base. And you cannot grow a business in a social vacuum. You have to understand the dynamics of the market. Markets are not one color; they are a mosaic. You have to recognize that."

Linda Alvarado has seen the construction industry change over the years as she grew from being a small subcontractor to the major general contractor she is today. She has some definite thoughts on the subject of change: "People measure success very differently. My success has come from my ability to enable others—the people who work for me and with me—and to understand that change is constant. In order to be at the top of your game, you have to be able to adapt to change. The only reason I'm a success is I can empower those around me to meet our clients' expectations and make them understand that it's part of their dream also."

Rebecca Matthias has seen her business grow from a small catalogue venture being operated out of a spare bedroom into the world's largest manufacturer and retailer of maternity clothing. At every step along the way, she faced challenges and the need to adapt and to change:

> I think every business goes through stages. You have the start-up stage where you have a great idea—it's very exciting and you get started. You then enter your toddler years where you start to have problems like cash flow. They take you into the growing years where you really develop into a real business. Every stage has its own issues and its own challenges. If you follow your nose and you follow your business, the business will tell you where it's going and what it needs.
>
> When you first start, you can't really have a preconceived idea about what your business will look like 10 years later. You always have to have a plan, and you always have to have a goal, but you have to be flexible enough to change it as things change. My business went through various stages: we went from start-up as a mail-order catalog, to offering franchises, to buying those franchises back and opening our own stores, to starting manufacturing because we couldn't find the products we were looking for. Every challenge represented an opportunity. If you're opportunistic, you can take every challenge and turn it into a solution that I think will allow your business to grow and expand and go in new directions.
>
> Never give up because you only fail when you stop trying. I wanted to stop probably 50 times when I was just getting my company started. But something or someone would force me to keep going and I found a way. If you just refuse to give up, your company will develop, but perhaps not the way you originally thought. In my case, I thought I'd have a mail-order catalog business, and I don't anymore. My business has changed and transformed so many times. You might change your mind about what it is that you have to stay in the game.

LuLu Sobrino whose dessert company went from supplying a few local markets to supplying wholesale distributors around the world couldn't agree more.

"When times change, you need to change," she says. "You had better be able to change your mentality and say, "I am not just going to continue doing things the old-fashioned way I have been doing them and I really need to move to the next level. I'm really open for possibilities."

6

Seek an Edge by Finding Your Niche

The conventional wisdom is represented by the expression "Don't reinvent the wheel." For the prospective small business owner, that means don't go out there and start a new business that is simply a carbon copy of what is already out there.

If you plan to open an Italian restaurant in an area where there are already several thriving Italian restaurants, you had better offer something that will cause restaurant goers to desert those places for yours. Maybe it is a different style of cooking, maybe it's a lower price point, or maybe it's a more glamorous dining experience. But it has to be something different and hopefully better.

During my years in Washington, DC, I lived in an area where there are a huge number of restaurants. They came and went with a frightening frequency. When one went under, seemingly a weekly occurrence, within a matter of weeks someone was redecorating the space in anticipation of opening a new eating establishment.

I was constantly amazed that someone would, as an example, open a new Thai restaurant when within a four-square block area there were already three other Thai restaurants. This is especially true when, after this new restaurant opened, you were hard-pressed to find any difference from the established restaurants.

One day I noticed that a new Italian restaurant was opening literally in the same block as two other Italian restaurants. I was dumbfounded that the owner of the new place would risk the kind of money he was obviously investing on the chance he could lure diners from the other two places, or the half dozen other Italian restaurants within a mile or so. The new place did not seem to be offering a different style of Italian cooking, nor was it more of a down-home mom-and-pop-style eatery with lower prices than the other two. Nor, for that matter, was it more formal with starched tablecloths and white-tie service catering to a special event clientele.

It would be one thing if the owner had done a market survey and found that the other Italian restaurants were filled to overflowing every night and diners needed to make a reservation a month in advance if they hoped to get in on a Saturday night. In fact, my family was usually able to walk in off the street and be immediately seated in one of the other two restaurants. It might make some sense if we were talking about a neighborhood everyone calls "Little Italy"—and where there is always room for one more Italian restaurant.

But in the case of this new Italian restaurant, it appeared the owner just thought he had a better idea and was willing to bet his money—or his backer's money—that he can make a go of it. It will be interesting to see if he does.

The same holds true if you are opening a dry cleaner, or manufacturing a novelty item, or hanging out your shingle as an accountant or some other provider of professional services. How are you different? How will you be able to distinguish yourself from what's already out there?

Two of the most successful businessmen I know, Dimensions International, Inc.'s Bob Wright and Fabrica International's Al Frink, have both learned this lesson.

"One thing I learned a long time ago," says Wright, "is that to be successful you have to find a need and fill it. There are a lot of needs that are out there, and you have to find them and then fill them. You must create a niche for yourself and then just work your tail off to make it happen."

Frink puts it this way, "If you're starting a new business, whether it's producing a product or providing a service, you have to have something that you're doing that distinguishes you from what's already available. It's important to look for voids that are not currently being serviced in the marketplace. When you come into the marketplace, what is it that's going to define what you're going to do? Your long-term success is going to be defined by your ability to be different, unique, and better.

"The key is your ability to differentiate yourself in providing a service or making a product that will be your edge. If you can't enter a market with that, then you better wait until you can. How are you going to be able to succeed in the new venture if you can't define what you are going to do in terms of success?

"When I first started in the carpet industry, there were close to 10,000 carpet manufacturers in the United States alone. Today, there are less than 50. The company I founded is still one of them because it was positioned not to be a low-cost producer, but to differentiate itself."

So if finding your niche is the answer, the obvious question is how do you go about finding your niche?

Bill Bryan, a counselor with the Northern Illinois SCORE, gives some advice:

> The ultimate key to small business success is finding a niche that is not covered. If you can identify your own niche, you'll probably do well. We are all trying to do business in an overcrowded marketplace and soft economy.
>
> The consumer is inundated with commercial messages and often does not know which way to turn. Too many choices and too many sellers compete for a buyer's attention. It's enough to make some folks say, "To heck with it" and stay home with their consumer dollars.
>
> Finding a market niche—which you must defend by operating superbly and providing customer service without peer—is the secret for financial success.
>
> When a successful baseball player was asked for the secret to his constant batting success, he replied, "I hit 'em where they ain't."

SCORE has a wonderful device for teaching small business owners, or potential small business owners, many of the lessons they must absorb if they are to be successful. SCORE calls these lessons "60-Second Guides." They can be found at *http://www .score.org/guides.html*.

Jennifer Lawton founded a computer service company, and then became senior vice president for corporate strategy of a major Internet company and now has switched careers by buying Just Books, Inc., which she calls the "Smallest but Oldest Bookstore in Greenwich, Connecticut." She has written a number of incisive articles for the small business web site of the Ewing Marion Kauffman Foundation. Here is her interesting take on finding your niche and on niche marketing:

> I've learned that niche marketing can play two ways. The first, which is what we do, is to have a niche-oriented company that you support with marketing and other "branding" efforts. The second is to have a broad-based company that seeks new markets, or a deeper experience, within a specific piece of the broad market.
>
> One starts as a niche, the other carves a niche within a broader space. So when formulating your niche marketing campaign, you must first decide where you fit. Once you do, consider implementing the following five-point plan, which can play to either niche "face":
>
> 1. Know yourself.
> 2. Know your goal.
> 3. Know your customer.
> 4. Keep it simple.
> 5. Have fun!

Here's a tip for how to find a niche: If you need something and can't find it, do others need the same thing and can't find it either. If so, have you discovered a need, a market, a potential business?

I am amazed by some of America's most successful companies that are now household names that were started by entrepreneurs who first found a need because they personally had a need.

There's Tom Stemberg, who we talked about earlier, driving around the suburbs of Boston on a Fourth of July weekend looking for and not finding a printer ribbon. This led him to realize that office products were not being marketed correctly and that led him to the concept of the office superstore and the birth of Staples.

Another mega-successful entrepreneur, Rebecca Matthias of Philadelphia, had a personal need and realized that if she did, then others might as well. This realization led her to establish a small business in her home that has become a worldwide retailer.

In 2003, I had the great pleasure of awarding her the SBA's Woman Entrepreneur of the Year award. Her company, Mothers Work Inc., is an amazing success story that started because, well, she just didn't have anything to wear.

Rebecca Matthias graduated from Columbia with a degree in architecture and then went to MIT to get a degree in engineering. She got married, got pregnant, and saw her life change in a way she never for a moment had considered. She says:

> I was trained to be an architect and engineer. My first job out of college was as a construction engineer. I had on my hard hat, and I was walking around the construction site. That's where I met my husband who was the president of a start-up. He was constructing a building, and in 1980 I was hired to work on the project. That's when my eyes were first opened to the idea of starting my own business because he had started three or four businesses. We got married and moved to Boston, and he was starting up another company. I got pregnant and didn't know what I really wanted to do next so I thought I would help him with his business. And that's when I realized how exciting it was to start a business. So I decided that when the baby came, I'd start a business in my home.
>
> As my pregnancy progressed and I got bigger, I couldn't find maternity clothes to wear to work. Then I started thinking about what I was going to do after the baby was born and all these thoughts came together. Then one day, the lightbulb went on. I realized what I wanted to do was to start a business to sell maternity clothes to pregnant women who needed clothes for work. That's how I started my company. I started it as a mail-order catalog company out of my home.
>
> I put together this little mail-order catalog even though I didn't know what I was doing, which I guess was another asset that I had. I didn't have any preconceived ideas of what would work or what wouldn't work, so I just tried a lot of things. I think that's another entrepreneurial thing that people go through, just trial and error. It's no longer a theoretical thing when you start a company, you just have to go out there and pound the pavement, put the product on the market and see if people will buy it.

I found some products in the wholesale marketplace and although they weren't exactly what I was looking for—because my product wasn't really being made yet—I was able to find products that were close enough to what I wanted. I was able to put together this little catalog. I used the Yellow Pages to find all my suppliers, like a photographer and a printer, and I picked a couple of national media outlets I thought my customers would be reading, and put in these little one-inch ads. My first ad just said, "Work Pregnant?" and my address to send for a catalog. It caught a lot of people's attention, and they wrote in for the catalog and I had a really strong response.

The new maternity clothing business started to slowly expand, and as it did, Rebecca began to think of ways she could begin growing the fledgling company:

I stayed in the catalog business for a year or two and built it up, and then realized that if I was going to keep growing I had to get into direct retail. The first retail stores I opened were all franchised and that was because I didn't have the expertise and I thought through franchising I could get partners who would help me. I didn't have the money, and franchisees would put up their own money. I got up to 20 to 25 franchised stores in a short period of time. That was another advantage of franchising—we could grow rapidly.

I named the company Mothers Work because it was for new mothers who had to work. Over time that changed, and I got into many different kinds of maternity clothing, not just career clothing. The business grew and just took off.

Took off is probably more than a bit of an understatement. Started in 1982 as a catalog business, Mothers Work, Inc. has grown to become the world's largest maternity apparel retailer with more than 1,500 locations. Since the time of its initial public offering in March 1993, Mothers Work has added many new stores, acquired existing maternity stores, established new brands, and increased sales volume.

In its first 10 years, the company grew to $31 million in sales volume. By 1999, it grew tenfold to $300 million and since then has doubled again doing $602 million last year. Rebecca says:

I needed business clothes to wear to work and figured if I had that need, other women did also. I like to say that the best new businesses are started by people who have a need, and then they realize that other people have the same need and they go about crafting the business that addresses those needs. I think maybe that's the best way to start a business—by looking within your own needs and realizing that other people have that need also.

That's what really got me started—wanting to start a business and then finding a product to sell. I would advise anyone who wants to start a business to look at her life, what does she need and use, what need does she have that isn't being served well, whether it's a product or a service. If you have a need, there are probably other people who have that need also. You may well be able to somehow turn that into a business, to understand as a consumer what product is needed. And that's very important for any business—to understand the needs of the customer. So one thing I tell people to do if they're thinking about starting a business is to think about the products and services they need in their own lives and then to think about translating that into a business.

Looking at your own needs is a great way of discovering a product or service that others might need. Filling that need might turn into a business.

Tom Stemberg couldn't find a printer ribbon and that led to Staples. Rebecca Matthias didn't have a thing to wear and that led her to becoming the largest maternity clothing manufacturer and retailer in the world. For Steve Leveen and his wife Lori, their business idea was born the night they realized they didn't have a good enough lamp to both read by in their poorly lit condominium in the Boston suburb of Belmont.

It was 1987 and Steve was working in marketing for a software firm in Boston. You probably could not have found a couple less likely to become entrepreneurs. Steve had an undergraduate degree in biology from the University of California, San Diego, and he had earned his master's and doctoral degrees in sociology from Cornell University. Lori graduated from Vassar College with honors in history and earned her master's in international business from Georgetown University. They had scrimped and saved and bought themselves a house. The first evening they sat in the living room of their new home to read, they saw immediately they had a problem. As Lori puts it:

> There we were in our new living room, in the house we'd stretched for, and there wasn't enough light so both Steve and I could read. We started joking around, fighting for the seat next to Grandma's old dinosaur floor lamp. Then it dawned on us.

Steve was aware of a new product that was just emerging—the halogen lightbulb. So he searched out a lamp utilizing this new lighting source and found it met his and Lori's needs. They now both could read at the same time. Then they thought if they had this need for a better reading light, others might also. He says:

> We looked around and saw that a revolution of sorts had just begun in lighting technology. At the time, though, few people—few Americans, at least—were aware of this new type of lightbulb called halogen. It would be, we decided, an excellent source of lighting for serious readers.
>
> We put several lamps together in our first booklet. It would be generous to call it a catalog, since it was really a folded piece of paper. We thought there might be a market for this new halogen lightbulb, so we put a couple of small ads in the New York Times and Boston Globe that didn't do anything, but one in the New Yorker did. We found we had a very responsive audience there, especially for a light for reading.

They offered "Serious Lighting for Serious Readers" and they began to get phone calls:

> We talked to customers from our call center—in the spare bedroom. The fulfillment center was first our den, then a neighbor's garage. Lori and I pooled our retirement funds, sold our first new car—a 1985 Mitsubishi Montero—and with the money we netted, combined our surnames of Granger and Leveen to form Levenger, Inc.
>
> Listening to customers is critical when you start a business and critical every step of the way. Our customers were very interested in the lighting for reading, particularly for reading in bed, and that's where we focused because that's where our customers wanted us to focus. One of our most important products starting off was a light for reading in bed. It was actually designed for technicians putting together electrical components, but it turned out that a focused halogen light was also wonderful for reading, particularly for one person to read in bed, while the other was trying to sleep.

The company grew and it began to offer what it called "Tools for Serious Readers." Steve admits:

> Marketing scholars of today might congratulate us for finding a niche market so quickly—but at the time, that's not how we saw it. We simply listened to our customers and adapted. They told us they wanted good chairs and desks and other reading accessories.

Eventually, the company moved to Florida—with both of its employees—and over the past almost 20 years became first a major catalog company offering a wide range of products, and then an established Internet presence. More recently, Levenger has opened retail stores in some high-class shopping malls and emporiums.

As I mentioned earlier in Chapter 3, I had the good fortune of working with the most dynamic women entrepreneur I have even known, my deputy administrator at the SBA, Melanie Sabelhaus.

Melanie came to the SBA after a long career, first as a marketing leader at IBM, and then as a hugely successful leader of an industry she essentially invented because one day she had a need she could not fill and figured, quite correctly, if she had such a need that others must also and, well, I'll let her tell you her own story:

> I'm from Cleveland, Ohio, and my dad was a steelworker and my mother was a homemaker, and neither had been able to go to college so they insisted that I would be able to go. They told me, "You're going to be anything you want to be." So I went to Ohio University. This was the greatest thing. There was a busboy in our sorority house who was working three jobs so I thought he was quite a catch and I snatched him. That was Bob Sabelhaus, and that was 32 years ago.
>
> My first job was at Sears and being a college graduate I asked them if I could get into their management-training program. They said "Absolutely," and after I tested for it, they told me I could be a management trainee in the wig department. So my very first job was as a management trainee selling wigs. You might say, "Oh my, this for a college graduate," but for me it was great because what I learned was—I could sell. I didn't sell one wig to ladies who walked in; I sold them two or three and all the accessories that went with them. I became the top wig salesperson at Sears.
>
> From that job, the doors opened for me. I told an IBM recruiter that if I could sell wigs, I could sell computers. So I ended up at IBM for a fabulous 15-year career. At one point, I had a temporary assignment in New York City at the Madison Avenue Product Center as the manager of the Center, selling, for the first time, what we were calling a personal computer.
>
> Bob was working for Merrill Lynch at the time and we both thought our assignments would be temporary. So I asked a realtor if she could find us a furnished townhouse or large apartment or house to live in until we could see how long we would be in New York. The answer I got was, "There's nothing like that available, everything I have are on leases of one year or more, and they're all unfurnished."
>
> So I thought, "Aha! This is an opportunity."
>
> Based on my own need, I could not find a product. So I did what any smart woman would do, I moved us—the kids and the nanny—into the Plaza Hotel and we lived there for almost three months. I wanted a coffee

machine, but all they had was room service. I wanted a washer and dryer, but I could only send laundry out. So I thought if I had this need, if my husband and I and our family have this need, how many others must also?

This was essentially a "tire kicker" experience. If I needed it, and it wasn't available, why not start it?

When we relocated to Baltimore, Maryland, once again we could not find upscale furnished housing, so I said, "Bob, I want to start this kind of business."

He supported me 100 percent. So there I was, an IBM manager in Baltimore, trying this business on the side because I kept my day job—which I recommend strongly. By this time, we had bought a home, and I took our guesthouse, furnished it completely with everything from a Mr. Coffee to linens, china, and utensils, and ran an ad: "Corporate relocation suite available complete with maid service—just bring your toothbrush."

I got an immediate response from an executive who wanted to get out of a downtown hotel. I charged him a premium, but it was great for him to get out of the hotel and have space for his family to come and visit on the weekends, and I immediately knew I was on to something.

One of the first things my tenant asked me was, "When does the maid service start?" Well, I didn't have a maid, so I became the maid and essentially learned my business from the ground up. After about eight months, I thanked IBM for a wonderful 15-year career and said I was setting out on my own business.

The year was 1986, and Melanie called the new company Exclusive Interim Properties Ltd. (EIP). It just grew and grew. Its big leap forward came when it opened an office in nearby Washington, DC, probably the nation's biggest market for temporary housing. At its peak, EIP had offices in Baltimore and Washington, DC, owned 650 furnished units ranging from apartments to townhouses to detached single-family homes, employed 75 people, and generated some $12 million annually. Melanie says:

Finally, we had been in business for 13 years, and we were beginning to see competition. We clearly had the best product around, but we started to see the suite concept beginning in long-stay hotels, which really was different from what I was offering—townhouses, apartments, and homes—but I thought this would be the perfect time to try to consolidate with other firms that were doing what I was doing. I found four like companies with excellent reputations and we joined together, called ourselves Bridgestreet Accommodations, and did a rollup and an IPO. We went public on the NASDAQ in 1997 and our IPO was six times oversubscribed. We raised roughly $60 million and we were an overnight success.

Finding your niche, whether by research or by simply finding that you personally have a need and then extrapolating that others might have the same need is fine, but to make the leap from there to establishing a business puts you up against what might be called the *green widget dilemma.*

Say you have determined that no one in your area is selling green widgets. The key question is does anyone want to buy green widgets? You may become the area's only green widget maker, but if everyone is buying only blue widgets, then you are going to have a very big problem.

Dan F. Sturdivant, who we meet at greater length later, is the assistant to the director of the Department of Homeland Security's Office of Small and Disadvantaged Business Utilization. He is one of the deans of the government's small business initiative and one of the federal government's top procurement experts.

He calls the problem "niche versus need." It comes down to your niche versus the customer's need. In terms of selling to the Department of Homeland Security, it comes down to whether your niche meshes with his need. Sturdivant says:

> No federal agency buys everything. People say Homeland Security must have a voluminous procurement budget and we have. In fiscal year 2005, we bought almost 48 percent from small business and our goal is 25 percent. But we don't buy everything. I don't buy widgets. So if you're selling widgets, your niche doesn't meet my need.

This warning, of course, has a much broader application. It's not just that a particular buyer might not have a need for your product; it's that no buyer, or not enough buyers, will have a need to justify starting a business. Finding your niche is all well and good—and it certainly was for Tom Stemberg, Rebecca Matthias, and Steve and Lori Leveen—but you must also spend whatever time you need determining if there is a market out there for what you want to do.

Part of seeking an edge by finding your niche comes from learning about what works in your business. I've heard it described as *your distinct competitive advantage.*

For example, if you lose a customer, thank them for the opportunity to do business with them. Don't burn the bridge and don't get mad, be grateful. They gave you a chance. Sometimes they will come back or appreciate your character and refer other business to you. At the very least, they can give you the opportunity to find out why they are leaving so you can learn from the experience.

Examples of this are Lulu Sobrino, who found a niche that wasn't being met in the gelatin dessert category, or Tom Stemberg, who found a way to offer office supplies on a mass scale. They both did so in a cost-effective and efficient manner before anyone else was doing it on the same scale. It is often said that necessity is the mother of invention, but just because something is needed, or works, does not mean it will sell.

I like the concept of enrollment that I learned years ago: "What does that mean for me?" It reminds me that no one likes a hard sell, but everyone likes to be invited. Instead of demanding that someone buy something from you because you really need to sell it to them, you should find a way to offer them an opportunity to benefit from a product or service that they need.

It is the difference between calling someone and demanding that they show up for dinner at your place, as opposed to telling them it would be an honor if they would consider having dinner at your home as your guest. It makes all the difference in the world and can lead to much more favorable results.

In addition, people will stop doing business with you if they think you take them for granted. They will ultimately go somewhere else. Part of being in business is the practice of retention, keeping an existing client happy. It is much less expensive and easier to keep an existing client happy than to find a new one. You must guard your customers, and surround them zealously with benefits, and maintain the highest level of service if you are going to keep them in the long run.

When I started my sales career, I learned that you must first sell those customers what they want, and then sell them what they really need—not the other way around. I remember learning the saying, "People don't care what you know until they know you care." I know this to be true.

7

The Key Is the People around You

"People are your most precious resource." I heard this consistently time and time again from most of the entrepreneurs interviewed for this book. If you talk with enough successful small business owners who have gone on to become large business owners, one thing that stands out is their humbleness. It's usually easy to tell when humbleness is put on, when someone is thinking, "Yeah, I really am great but it sounds phony, so I'm going to pretend I really don't believe it." But often when you talk with those who have made it, and made it big, what you hear over and over is that their success is a function of the hard work and dedication of those around them. It is a measure of their ability that they found and then motivated the people around them and it is their ability to impart to those people their vision that is primarily responsible for their success. But almost to the person, they seem to genuinely believe that it has been the shared hard work, the shared vision, and the shared experience with their employees that has led them down the road to success.

You might say, "It's the people around you, stupid!" You hear it enough and those you hear it from obviously believe it, so it has the ring of truth. These successful people obviously believe it, so you have to believe that a central factor in success is finding, hiring, and motivating people to share your vision. What you hear time after time is that when your business is very small, you may be able to do much of the work yourself. But as your business begins to grow, you're going to have to bring people on board not only simply to help but also to complement you and your skills. Then you must—and I stress *must*—delegate responsibilities to these people if your enterprise is to grow and prosper.

The importance of people is indisputable, as is the importance of any successful business owner's ability to lead them. I have often said, in my business and as the head of a government agency with thousands of employees, that it is impossible to accomplish anything significant by yourself, especially at the SBA when we were breaking records every year. But I wasn't the one who was approving loans or training business owners or giving government contracts to deserving qualified small businesses. It was the thousands of people who worked at the SBA, or with the SBA, and all of the countless partners and supporters who made those accomplishments a reality.

I used to say that it was easy to get credit for the incredible achievements we were experiencing when I had so many people working beside me who did all of the heavy lifting. The value of good people has been true in all of the organizations and initiatives that I have been fortunate enough to be involved with.

Linn Wiley is one of California's premier bankers. His many years in banking and in dealing with a wide variety of small businesses have driven this point home.

"I think I'm a success because of the terrific people I have been able to attract," Wiley says. "It's all about the people. For any leader, it's about the people around him. There's not much a *single person can do; it takes the support of the people around* him."

Earlier we met Fred Ruiz whose business Ruiz Foods has grown into one of the largest prepared foods companies in the country. Over the 43 years he has been in business, he has learned some very valuable lessons in how to run a successful business. He says:

Another important lesson that I learned was you can be in the right place at the right time with an incredible product, but if you don't have the people you won't be able to fully capture the opportunity. I think people are a major force in any business. When you can get people motivated and have faith in what you're trying to do, it's amazing how much power there is and what a positive force it can be. When you bring people together and everyone is focused, you have a tremendous competitive advantage. It requires communication, organization, and rewarding people for their effort.

I think I'm a success because of the people I've worked with and, in some part, because I really didn't know what I was doing or what I was getting into. You're just thrust into it and you have to find a way through it; there's no turning back. You just have to take the attitude that I'm going to figure it out, and then you just do it.

In the early years, it was so difficult getting people to understand our issues and then getting them on board to work with us to find a solution. But if you can create an environment of trust and get people on board, you can incentivize those people by getting them to believe you're doing the right thing and then reward them for their hard work, I cannot over-emphasize how important that is.

Bob Lotter, who we have met briefly, is one of the great business success stories I know. He started out 20-plus years ago selling insurance out of his house and since has built R.A. Lotter Financial Group and eAgency into an insurance and financial powerhouse that has written over a billion (that's billion with a B) dollars worth of insurance. Lotter says:

I've gone through a lot of transitions over the years. I've written over a billion dollars in premiums over the years and still write in the hundreds of millions. At times, I had thousands of agents working for me around the country. Now we've changed in that we are not interested in mass numbers of agents but rather in concentrating on the few hundred who are real quality and we have changed the business into a lifestyle-type business.

We've started a publishing company and a technology company, and I travel abroad to consult quite a bit.

Bob Lotter sees himself as a people person:

I'm a pretty self-critical person, so I keep a long list of mistakes I've made. The biggest types of mistakes I've made are mistakes where I became impatient with others. I've had to learn that this kind of impatience costs me a relationship with a person or causes me to make things more difficult for myself. But I guess I haven't made any serious blunders, which I guess I should be happy about.

The bottom line of what I do is take people, many of whom have failed at things, and train them and nurture them to be successful. When you repeat this cycle over and over, you learn that a lot of people don't have the persistence—that when things get hard they go someplace else. I think that with persistence you can overcome any problem. You can get more education, you can try harder, you can learn a better way. If you're persistent, you can overcome whatever difficulty.

An important lesson I've learned is there are different kinds of capital in business. There is money, and then there are people. Bottom line, and I'm not the only one who has had this epiphany, the most important capital you can have is people. If you get the right people, things seem to happen and you have success. If you get the wrong people, then it's more difficult.

The way I look at things, there are two classes of people. There's the lazy person, perhaps mentally lazy, work ethic lazy, or someone who has a lack of persistence. Then there is the super aggressive person who only cares about money. The lazy person's problem is that he can never get anything done; he can't succeed because he can never stick with anything very long. The super aggressive person is money motivated, so all he cares about is money, money, money. He'll make all his decisions based on how much money he is going to get. He doesn't do any long-term planning.

Maybe it's something about the Bobs I know, but Bob Lotter is a phenomenal success, and so is Bob Wright.

Robert L. Wright is both a visionary and a pioneer. He was born in Columbus, Georgia, and earned a BS as well as an optometry degree from Ohio State University. In 1980, he was appointed associate administrator for Minority Small Business at the SBA by President Reagan. There he managed the Office of Minority Small Business/Capital Ownership Development, whose mission was to foster business ownership and promote competitive viability of eligible socially and economically disadvantaged businesses.

He left the SBA in 1983 and began doing some consulting. But then he decided rather than advising others, he would start a business himself.

"I've always been an entrepreneur," Bob Wright says. "I've been in business now 43 years. The only time since I finished college I didn't write my own check was the two years I spent at the SBA."

So in 1985, he started Dimensions International, Inc. as a three-person operation. When in June of 2007 he sold it to Honeywell for $230 million, it had grown into a $180 million annual operation with about 1,500 employees around the world working out of 30 offices providing what the company called "technological solutions to federal, military, and civilian agencies and commercial customers." Wright says:

> My first contract was with the SBA, and then I got a contract with the Department of Agriculture. It was a $1.8 million contract and it gave us our first entrée into doing business with the government. We began to grow, and eventually I was employing 20 to 25 people. Then we got a major $38 million contract with the Federal Aviation Administration. That really gave us traction because all of a sudden I had engineers and other skilled people coming into the company with a lot of technical know-how I didn't have. The challenge then became to manage these people, and at the same time grow the company.

Bob Wright has developed an interesting perspective on adding people to a growing company and the difficulties that startups on a tight budget sometimes have:

> When you're a small business, and just getting started putting a company together, you really can't afford to hire the best and brightest. So you really have to struggle with the second tier. I don't mean to be disrespectful to the people I hired then, but you really can't afford to hire the brightest or the people with the best experience. You hire people with little experience and you're trying to get to the next level, but they don't have the experience to get you there.
>
> So that's always a challenge for a new business managing through that aspect. Now, we can afford to hire the best and brightest and that's all we go after—people who understand how to price, how to market, how to go after the biggest contracts, and as a result we've been able to challenge some of the largest companies and win contracts. But you can't do that when you're small.

With experience, comes the ability to better choose and manage people, says Wright:

> Compared to when I first started out, I think I'm a better judge of people. At the same time, I think I'm less tolerant of people who are not performing. When you first start, you have to go along with people because they have you boxed in—you really can't afford to hire anyone else. I think if I had to do it all over again, in some instances, I would cut my losses much quicker and move on a lot quicker.

Most small business owners, almost by definition, are type-A personalities and one of the principal traits of type-A personalities is the belief that they can do it all themselves. In a growing small business situation, that can be very dangerous.

Mercedes LaPorta, who has built her electrical supply business in Miami into a major player in the South Florida marketplace and who often counsels women who are small business owners, says she sees the danger often.

She says, "A major mistake I see small business owners make is not having the right kind of people around them. I often see them trying to do everything by themselves, not delegating, not knowing when to step back and give their people the responsibility so that they can concentrate on what they do best. The small business owner must put their resources where they are most needed. The owner has only so much time and must put it to the best use."

Mercedes uses herself as an example: "I understand what I do best is sell and represent my company to my customers. I am not a backroom kind of person. I am not an accountant or inventory expert. So I have people to run those parts of my business so I have time to do what it is I do best, sell."

"For a growing business, a big mistake I see often is not adding enough middle management talent soon enough," says Linda Alvarado, the Colorado construction leader. "Entrepreneurs some-times think 'we're entrepreneurs' and we don't need anyone. But the truth is as your business grows you need people who can help you sell and help you manage. You have to be able to show you have people in your organization who can deliver because you can't be there 100 percent of the time.

It's critical that as a new business adds workers that they possess not only strengths and abilities that perhaps the business' founder doesn't, but also that can add diverse voices and thinking as the business grows and moves forward. This is something on which both LaPorta and Alvarado agree.

"Another big mistake growing business owners make is hiring only people who think exactly like they do," warns Alvarado. "We need people who can challenge us. You can't just have a bunch of yes people. You need people who can challenge and add perspec-tive. Even within your own organization, you can have conven-tional thinking and that prevents the likelihood of growth."

LaPorta couldn't agree more, "A small business owner must not be afraid to bring people into the business with strengths and opinions that are different from theirs. If you bring someone in who is very strong in a certain area, especially in an area that you are not very strong in, that will only add to the overall strength of your business and will not make you any less. If it's done properly, and you integrate this person correctly into your business, it's only going to enhance your business."

We will meet Hawaiian entrepreneur Thanh Quoc Lam at greater length in Chapter 8. He has overcome incredible challenges in his life to become the owner of a food and bakery empire that made him an SBA Entrepreneur of the Year. He says the key for a growing small business is finding good employees, training them well, and then treating them right. Thanh says:

> Every year since I opened in 1984 my business has continued to grow. My sales volume has gone up every year including this past year. I'm very lucky to have good employees. But you will lose good employees unless you treat them well. So I try to treat them well and to respect them. No matter how good you are as an owner, you need help, you need good people around you. My job is to go out, visit the accounts, and get the business. I don't make the food. That's up to my employees. If they don't do a good job, I can lose an account. It's a matter of teamwork. So I'm lucky to have good employees.

Thanh offers his employees every possible opportunity to succeed. He starts them at a rate higher than minimum wage. He provides zero-interest financing on loans to franchisees. He also stresses education, with an emphasis on learning English. To this end, he offers flexible working hours to encourage employees to attend classes.

Tom Stemberg who built the Staples empire from a bright idea that office supplies just weren't being sold the right way and from a single store, has some interesting ideas about employees. Tom agrees that you lose good employees unless you treat them well. In starting Staples, he found ways to turn employees into members of a team.

First of all, says Stemberg, "We never called them employees, we always called them associates. We all looked at it like we were partners and in this together." Then, he says, "you have to sell your concept to them and show them they'll be rewarded if you succeed.

"To get people attracted to what you're doing, you have to sell your vision. But unless you have a compelling vision—and you can be as good a salesman as there is—it won't do you much good. You need to get your people incredibly excited about what you're doing and give them an incentive by giving them stock or stock options so that they will realize that they can make this work; it can change their lives."

That his associates were there with him was proven one day shortly after he opened his second store. He was driving with his young son on a Saturday afternoon when they began to see the fire engines. He quickly realized those fire engines were headed toward the store. He had only two stores at the time and this fire could have ruined him. He remembers:

> It happened in the spring of 1987; we only had two stores open and operat-ing. This really could have shut us down. My employees all owned stock in the company; so to an extent, they were entrepreneurs, too. They worked all night Saturday, and all day Sunday and Sunday night; by 9:00 AM on Monday morn-ing, we were able to open on schedule. It was completely a team effort.

He also has something interesting to say—based on experi-ence—how you should go about hiring key people if you have a growing business He says:

> To me the secret is to hire ahead of yourself, if you're growing—for instance we went from $8 million to $20 million to $40 million to $100 million. If I hired somebody when we were at the $8 million level, by the time he under-stood the business, we were at the $20 million level and heading for $40 mil-lion. A year later, that person, say he or she was hired to be a marketing director for the $8 million business, was now the marketing director of a $100 million a year business. That person may not have been qualified to do the marketing job for a company of that size. So the trick is to try to figure out how you can hire ahead of the curve. How, in fact, can you hire a marketing executive for the $120 million business, when you're still doing $20 million?
>
> While you're doing this, you will also have to convince him that as the company grows his job is going to have to get both narrower and deeper. For example, let's say I hired someone as director of merchandis-ing. She is going to do all the merchandising for a $20 million company. I'll tell the person that she can expect her job and responsibilities to grow and grow, but once they reach a certain level she probably won't be in charge of buying for the entire store, but rather maybe only a half or a third of the store. But, I tell her, "Your job will be much bigger than the one you started with." You need to get the person to buy into this at the very beginning; otherwise, you get people who, when you split up their job, become very unhappy and leave.

Melanie Sabelhaus, my former deputy administrator at the SBA, who started her furnished temporary housing business in her guesthouse in Baltimore and built the business to 650 units before taking it public, also found out how important it is to get the right people and then give them the incentives to help them share your vision and have a stake in helping you reach your goals. She says:

> You have to be sure you hire the right people to be around you. Not necessarily the best people, but the right people. You get the right people on the bus with you, and then together you figure out where you're going.
>
> People will always support what they helped create. If they're all part of the plan, if they all believe in the business, if they all share the vision and are all passionate, then together you're all driving forward, and you're going to be very successful.
>
> You must make sure that you recognize your employees and their contributions and pay them for their performance. You can't give everyone equal paychecks because you might have a person who comes in at nine and leaves at five. But you want their hearts and souls in it, because the more they sell the more they're going to get paid; and the better your customer satisfaction, the more they're going to get paid. You must give them the incentive. That's what makes people live up to their highest potential. You set the bar high, and then you compensate people who reach it.

David Lizarraga, who heads TELACU, agrees with the others. His success is based on those he has around him. He feels he is a success because of the team he has assembled. You can't accomplish anything by yourself; you need many good people around you.

"The biggest mistake I have made in business was, from time to time, bringing in the wrong people. But of course, you don't know they are the wrong people at the time. It's something you only learn in hindsight. You learn through trial and error to be a better judge of people, especially which people will be able to work within the culture of the organization."

So, what should a new business owner look for when hiring? We meet Linn Wiley, one of California's top bankers and a long-time advisor and lender to small businesses, at length later, but he has developed some definite ideas about hiring. He told me:

> We look for superior people. Superior people have four key qualities. Number one is teamwork and a commitment to teamwork; really focusing on the team and subordinating your own interests to that of the team.

You ask people if they really feel that teamwork is the best approach to achieving maximum results, everyone will say yes. They will embrace teamwork, and they will continue to embrace teamwork, until something doesn't go their way. And that's when teamwork starts to break down and, since no group of people is going to think the same way all the time, that is the challenge of teamwork. Usually we react on the basis of what's best for us individually, so we let ourselves as individuals get in the way of teamwork.

The second is commitment.

The third is integrity. I think ethics and integrity are integral to having a superior organization. Because anything less than that gets in the way of success.

The fourth thing is flexibility.

My own experience with family businesses is that the first impulse is to hire family and friends to take the jobs, especially the critical ones, in the company. It doesn't matter if it is the right fit or the right skill set. It also doesn't matter if the family member even wants the job, if it's their dream, or if they may resent you for putting them in that position.

Running a business is hard, and that's why you need the best people you can get. You need to give people incentives, you must respect your employees, and together you must have fun. Often, the reason family members are hired is because that is all that the small business can afford. And often, those family members are working for little or nothing at all. That was certainly the case in my family. We had to work together just to survive. It got easier as the business grew and became successful, but it was never easy.

It is critical that there be a serious commitment to execution when dealing with employees—in other words, the effective ability to get things done. It is also important to have accountability from the top down, holding someone accountable for what he says he would do is critically important to the health and viability of any enterprise.

Another trait must be honesty—being able to trust and count on those people who you are working with.

Larry Bossidy and Ram Charan in their book *Execution: The Art of Getting Things Done* (New York: Crown, 2002) talk about the importance of personnel and the fact that senior managers and executives cannot delegate that critical responsibility to a human resources department. Jim Collins, who wrote *Good to Great: Why Some Companies Make the Leap and Others Don't* (New York: HarperCollins, 2001), talks about getting the right people on and off the bus. Sometimes people will come, and sometimes they will go, but all are a part of the chain of that business's history. Obviously, you want people to stay as long as possible, especially if they're contributing to the mission. You must appreciate their contribution while they're making it. It fosters loyalty to the management and, of course, to the company.

Above everything, you must involve your employees in the business and make them part of a real team. A part of that is being honest with them, which will always pay dividends.

I met a business owner who was struggling trying to convince his employees that he didn't have more money to give them. So he called them all into the conference room, and he put a hundred pennies in a jar. He told them that the pennies in the jar represented all of the revenue that their company was producing.

As he took pennies out of the jar, he explained to them what they represented in terms of expenses. He took out pennies for the cost of producing their product. He took out pennies to represent the costs of rent and other monthly expenses. He took out pennies that represented their salaries and benefits.

Finally, there were only three pennies left in the jar, and he told them that represented the company's net profit that their labor was generating every year. It was an eye-opening exercise in finance for the employees that helped them all be on the same page and focus on producing improved profits.

8

Disaster Always Looms—Survive the Potholes

You may not know his name, but Robert H. "Bob" Lorsch is a Los Angeles-based businessman, entrepreneur, and philanthropist. When I was SBA administrator, it was my honor to present Bob with the SBA's "American Spirit Award," one of the highest honors the government can present to someone from the private sector.

Bob is quite simply one of the smartest businesspersons I know. Many people have good ideas and have the ability and fortitude to ride those dreams and ideas to the heights of success. You have met some of these people and will meet more in this book. Bob goes beyond this. He might be called a serial success. He has taken one idea, built it into a thriving enterprise, and then moved on to a completely different idea, building that into a thriving success. He has repeated this process multiple times. But to me what makes Bob unique is the degree of adversity he has had to overcome on multiple occasions to have been able to attain these successes. He started out without the advantages of a prestigious college degree—in fact, without any college degree, and he has had to overcome disasters, both natural and financial, during almost 40 years in business. But he has always rebounded—which is why he serves as a model for any businessperson facing difficulties that seem overwhelming.

From every corner when he was young, Bob was being told that he would not succeed. You could almost say he was given a ready-made path to failure. But he never took it, he says:

> Whether it was teachers or family members, I was constantly told I was going to fail. My cousins were going to Johns Hopkins, to UCLA, to all the great schools around the country, and I could barely get out of high school.
>
> I have taken a path that is different than what my teachers and the system wanted me to do. I wanted to go outside the system. When I was 14 years old, I didn't know that was what was going on in my head. But rather than being congratulated for thinking out of the box, I was punished for getting poor grades.

Without a college degree, Bob started out as an assistant produce manager in a grocery store, but he soon realized that he should accept the advice of nineteenth-century newspaper publisher Horace Greeley for the ambitious: "Go West, young man." When he was 18 years old, he loaded his car and set out for Los Angeles.

With only a paper-thin resume, he went to a recruiting firm that noted that he had the ability to sell himself, and they guessed he might be able to also sell other people's products, so they sent him to interview at an ad agency.

Bob remembers, "The ad agency asked how I would market these rubber stamps and I came up with the idea of marketing them at retail locations throughout the country with a coupon system." They hired him, and he soon was the national sales and marketing manager for X-Stamper, a self-inking rubber stamp company.

Bob was on his way to being an entrepreneur. But, as he laughingly says today, he had no idea what that was.

"I just always wanted to make money. I was willing to do anything that was within a legal or ethical framework that I believed in to make a buck. In order to make a buck and to be able to exceed what you can normally make in a salaried environment—unless you are willing to devote your life to one organization—you have to be willing to do it on your own. It's very, very difficult to get a job that will allow an individual to fulfill their financial dreams unless you are really, truly in the right place at the right time—the Horatio Alger story of starting in the stockroom and ending as the CEO of a multibillion-dollar enterprise."

If you look back over Bob Lorsch's varied career, it seems almost as if he thrives on adversity, that he sees disasters as challenges that have to be met head-on and overcome. Look at how he started, with barely a high school degree. Without a college degree, Lorsch looked for some field where formal education was not a prerequisite. Given his gift for selling himself and selling the products of others, the almost natural choice was advertising and marketing. In 1970, he founded Marketing Plus, a boutique marketing and advertising firm. He was 20 years old at the time. In 1975, the company was merged with another small advertising agency, and he soon bought out his partner. The company became the Lorsch Creative Network. This was his business for almost 25 years.

Soon Bob was representing small businesses and large. Clients like American Izusu Motors, Caesar's Palace, Johnson & Johnson, Van de Kamp's Foods, Procter & Gamble, Taco Bell, and, at times, three of the four major television networks. He says, "The more people told me I would fail, the more I just had to succeed. But eventually I realized that simply trying to prove people wrong for giving me a hard time on the way up was taking energy and focus away from what I had to do. It was somewhere in the process of Lifespring training that I came to the realization that wanting to get even was a waste of both time and energy. Once I got over wanting to get even, I got much more laser-focused and it was about that time that I was able to exceed even my own wildest imagination for wealth."

What makes Bob Lorsch so unusual is not that he worked hard and made a fortune and in doing so overcame unusual hardships and the low expectations of those around him. Others have done that, many of whom we have and will meet in these pages. But what makes Bob Lorsch stand apart is that he has made fortunes, lost fortunes, given away fortunes, and then done it all over again.

In 1994, a natural disaster struck, and with it came a whole new degree of adversity that would certainly have sunk a lesser man. At 4:30 AM, on January 17, 1994, residents of the greater Los Angeles area were rudely awakened by the Northridge earthquake. With a

Richter scale magnitude of 6.7, the ground acceleration was the highest ever recorded in an urban area in North America. It would prove to be the most costly earthquake in U.S. history. Bob's company had its offices on the top floor of a suburban office building near the quake's epicenter. In an instant, he was wiped out. Bob recalls:

> We had considerable damage and the building was shut down so the only option was to relocate the business to my home. But my home was also devastated. I needed disaster relief from the SBA to rebuild my home. In the course of getting those loans, my SBA counselor asked what I was going to do about my business. I was at a bit of a loss because in the wake of a disaster like this, no one in business was focused on spending money on advertising or marketing. I had to continue to pay my people, but I wasn't collecting my receivables so it was a very, very difficult time for me.
>
> It was only through an emergency loan to the business in addition to a personal loan that we were able to repair my home, which allowed me to keep the office open in the second story above the garage, and keep my people working.

Bob's trademark has been whenever he has been dealt lemons he has always been able to make lemonade. It happened again that summer when a client came to the struggling company and asked Bob to write a business plan for a new venture. It was once again Bob's innate ability to see the marketability of a product that rescued him. He remembers:

> A client named Mid-Com asked me to write a business plan involving enhanced telecommunications services. Had I still been shut down from the earthquake like so many others, I wouldn't have been there to do this.
>
> One of the segments of the proposed business was a service offering prepaid (telephone) calling cards for business. I didn't think what they were proposing was going to work, so I came back to them and said I thought it would only work in a retail market, selling from 7-Elevens and electronics stores and the like. They said, "Look we're a business to business company and we don't want to do that." So I said, "Do you mind if I go ahead and execute the prepaid calling card idea on a consumer level?" They said they didn't mind so long as I used their service to the extent they could provide it.

Thus, SmarTalk TeleServices, Inc. was born with a $5,000 investment. Bob now calls it his greatest accomplishment.

Lorsch was able to buy chunks of phone time from major carriers and resold it through the cards. It was an overnight sensation—remember, prepaid phone cards were a new item in the mid-1990s. As part of its subsequent expansion, SmarTalk purchased Boston-based SmarTel Communications Inc., another prepaid phone card firm, and then acquired GTI Telecom Inc. for $70 million. Then another kind of disaster struck, Bob says:

> In 1996, I woke up one morning in July and I had a huge lump in my neck. I went to the doctor and was told it was either an infection that had attacked my pituitary gland or it was cancer. I was about to head out on a road show for the SmarTalk initial public offering (IPO) and if I told anybody I was sick and might have cancer, the underwriters would have pulled the deal. But I was told if I didn't postpone my travel plans and go for the biopsies I might die. So I had to make the choice as to whether I would go through with the IPO and ignore the symptoms that might be cancer or have the biopsy and give up my dream.
>
> I went with the dream, with the IPO. We raised $60 or $70 million in a $300 million valuation; ultimately, without that money SmarTalk wouldn't have happened the same way.
>
> The minute I got off the road show, I went in for the biopsy and fortunately it was just an infection. Ironically, it turned out that in 2000 that infection did evolve into cancer and I ended up having massive surgery and now I'm okay.

Lorsch sold his interest in the company in 1998 when it had a market cap of close to $1 billion and after the new management team had a few setbacks, it was eventually sold to AT&T for close to a half-billion dollars.

"I founded the company with $5,000 in the bank in October 1994—money I had because an SBA loan had kept me in business, and soon I had a company with almost a quarter of a billion dollar market cap, and then it grew and grew." Lorsch says with a smile, "That is a growth story."

Earthquakes, investment reversals, lack of capital, illness—all were obstacles that might have defeated other businesspeople, but they didn't stop Bob Lorsch. In the process, they allowed him to develop an interesting way of viewing adversity.

"Obstacles are only as big as you make them," Lorsch says as he relates how a lawsuit that was filed against him early in his career threw him for a loop but that he got through it and learned from the experience:

Today, if somebody were to hit me with a lawsuit that has the potential of destroying my life, I simply would not allow that to happen. I would just hand it to my attorney, trust I have the right insurance coverage, and go on with my life.

If you visualize a train going down a track and the train goes off the track, that's a massive train wreck. We're no different. If we get off track, it's a train wreck, and it can take months, even years, to get back on track. So as these things come at you, you can't let them make you lose sight of where you're going.

Today, Lorsch is chief executive officer of the RHL Group, Inc., a business management and investment-holding corporation with interests in a number of companies including Campbell Soup Company, Procter & Gamble, Taco Bell, McDonalds, and others. More important, he is deep into another unique venture: *www.MyMedicalRecords.com*, an online service that provides an ultra-safe virtual vault and system where anyone can store their medical records and other important papers on a password-protected secure computer system and have them available 24/7 365 days a year from any computer in case of an illness or a crisis. As he was with prepaid phone cards in the 1990s, Lorsch is again ahead of the curve. The federal government is on its way to spending billions to ensure that within a decade everyone has an electronic medical record that is easily accessed and easily transferred. MyMedicalRecords.com is providing a solution today.

Many of the inductees in the SBA Hall of Fame are case studies in surviving a disaster or a deep pothole at the very least. You have met and will meet many of these people: Linda Alvarado, Bob Wright, Earl Graves, Harold Doley, and Tom Stemberg—all have compelling stories about overcoming adversity.

One of my favorite entrepreneurial ladies, Gert Boyle, cofounded Columbia Sportswear with her husband and had to carry on when he suddenly died. Earl Graves had to carry on when his boss, Senator Robert Kennedy, was assassinated. These are but a few of the dramatic examples of dealing with adversity and tragedy and going on to become an outstanding success despite a setback.

One of the major responsibilities of the SBA is providing assistance to small business owners after a natural disaster. My tenure, regretfully, was marked by two of the most significant disasters in U.S. history. The first was the 9/11 terrorist attacks that rocked our country and changed our world forever. The second was the most costly natural disaster in our history—Hurricane Katrina. During those trying times, I met some of the bravest and most inspirational people in my life. They happened to be small business owners.

I'll never forget Sal Iacona of New York City. He had a small store, by the name of "Sal the Sole Man" in Manhattan's financial district, in the shadows of the World Trade Center's Twin Towers. It was a shoe repair and shine store.

Sal told me that he went into his store the day after 9/11 and found it destroyed. There was trash, glass, and dirt everywhere. He began to clean up and turned the sign around that said, "Open for Business." He got to work, even though he knew that there would be no customers for a while. It was important for him to send a message to his community, customers, family, and country that he would not be denied the dream of having his own business.

He said to me, "Mr. Administrator, those terrorists thought they could declare a victory on our country by knocking down our World Trade Center. I worked so hard after the attack because I would not let them have a second victory by knocking me down and out of business."

The SBA was able to provide a small business loan to Sal and countless others to assist them back into business. Sal was able to open days after the attack. I went back to visit Sal on several occasions, and he never lost his spirit, commitment, or his passion for his business. I'm happy to say we were able to assist this special entrepreneur. He and many others contributed much to the spirit and inspiration that was so prevalent during those dark days in our nation's history.

I've heard it said that sometimes, when bad things happen, good things can come from it; we learned that many times after 9/11. It is one of the things that allows U.S. citizens to deal with hardship and come back stronger than ever. It is a quality that is always present with successful small business owners. It is one of the reasons that they are often described as the backbone of the U.S. economy.

I also vividly remember meeting a woman sometime later in Houston during one of our Business Matchmaking events. She said, "Mr. Administrator, you don't know who I am, but I want you to know that I am not a number or a statistic."

I wasn't sure what she meant. She said that after Hurricane Katrina she lost her business and was terrified that she would never be able to reopen. She said the hardest part was facing her employees, who she considered to be family, and telling them they may all lose their jobs. She said that, because of the SBA, and the loan that we provided, she was able to save her business and keep her employees. Now she was at this Business Matchmaking event, and we were helping her to make contacts so her business could grow.

By this point, she had tears streaming down her face, and she said, "I want you to know that I am a real-life person and that the programs and assistance that you have helped facilitate have made all the difference in the world." She was grateful and wanted me to know it.

I was humbled by her and explained to her that it was not me but the great people that I had the privilege of working with at the SBA who made those things happen. I assured her that I would never consider her a statistic or forget her. I thanked her for telling me what she did, so I could share it with all of the dedicated SBA employees.

I'm often asked who is the most successful entrepreneur I know. Truthfully, I know many people who have enjoyed great success. One, who has succeeded spectacularly and with amazing speed is Dallas-based Nina Vaca. She recovered rapidly from near disaster and also the horrible loss of family members.

For Bob Lorsch, it was a natural disaster—an earthquake—that put him and his company so deep in a hole. But for Nina Vaca, a nationwide financial earthquake almost ended her entrepreneurial dreams.

The year was 2001. The previous 18 months had seen the height of the dot-com frenzy, and then the beginning of the sharp reversal when the bubble burst.

Telecommunication companies were particularly hard hit. Leveraged up to their corporate eyeballs with mountains of debt from catastrophically rapid expansion, many began selling off assets or simply filing for bankruptcy. According to one authoritative compilation, at least 862 dot-com companies failed over the following 36 months.

Nina Vaca's five-year-old Pinnacle Technical Resources Inc. was almost in this latter category. Pinnacle was a professional services company that provided information technology (IT) personnel to technology companies, mainly to telecommunication companies.

Nina moved with her family from Quito, Ecuador, to Los Angeles when she was two years old. Her father, Hernan Alfredo Vaca, opened a travel agency, eventually expanding to five agencies, one each for his five children.

"My father believed that the key to the American dream was entrepreneurship," Vaca remembered in a recent interview. But shortly after Nina graduated from high school, her father was killed during a robbery at his travel agency. She and her older sister, Jessica, ran the business for a year while preparing it for sale.

Vaca says, "At 18, I was running a business, and it was then I understood what it really meant to run a business."

After the sale, Nina headed off for college, majoring in business at Texas State University and graduating in three and a half years with BAs in speech communications and business administration. She headed off to New York City to work for a technology company as an IT recruiter. She returned to Texas to head up its Dallas office. But the entrepreneurial genes were simply too ingrained in her and she decided to try it on her own. So in 1996, at the age of 25, she and a partner started Pinnacle to recruit IT talent for companies that needed technical personnel to manage their computer systems.

"The business started on the living room floor of my apartment," she remembers. "I was young and single at the time, and probably didn't know any better. I started the business in October of 1996 and didn't move the business out of my apartment and into office space until April 1, 1997. The company has changed dramatically in the 10 years since it was started."

The new business started in the twos: two partners, two employees, two phones, and two clients. By 2001, after almost five years in business, the company had grown steadily, reaching a revenue base of nearly $4 million with about 20 consultants. The company seemed poised to begin a growth spurt when the bubble burst. The bottom dropped out quickly and soon the company was contemplating implementing a liquidation plan Nina and her partner had drawn up. She was at a crossroads; commit to her company or let it go. She was determined to hold on and to ride out the storm. She says:

> The year 2001 was a very challenging year for us. We were faced with the downturn in technology; and the clients we were serving at the time were mainly in technology and telecommunications. We were down to four people in headquarters, and maybe had a total of 10 billable people overall.
>
> My partner said that if the company was to survive he would have to get out because he was too taxing on the meager resources we had. He needed to draw a salary, while I didn't because my husband was employed and I could get through without taking any money from the company. Besides, I was always of the mindset to reinvest whatever we made back into the company. So essentially my partner and I had different philosophies— take money out as we made it, or leave it in, and reinvest in the company.
>
> So my partner left and offered to sell me his percentage in the business. I took it. I borrowed money from everybody I could think of, the bank, my family, my friends, and used the money to buy half of essentially nothing. But it gave me 100 percent control of the firm, and from that point on I could do things my way.

Doing things her way radically changed the way the small company offered its services:

> We began to diversify and instead of delivering just one level of service, I added new lines of business. I was able to become a prime contractor instead of just a subcontractor, and with all the layoffs that were occurring in the technology industry there was a great deal of available talent—I was able to find the best. So armed with good talent, prime contracts, and new business lines, we were able to begin a period of growth.

Finding an appropriate adjective to describe Pinnacle's growth is difficult. Amazing, spectacular, dizzying, unbelievable—all come to mind. In just five years, from the doorstep of insolvency, Nina Vaca has grown her business more than 25-fold. She says:

> Today, we have four different lines of business: our client base is still the Fortune 500. We still provide them with IT talent, although today we do it in a variety of different ways. The company is still headquartered in Dallas, Texas, but today we have offices in Virginia, Los Angeles, Houston, and have more than 600 consultants in 23 major locations in the United States as we operate in 38 states. We will soon have close to 1,000 employees.

In 2007, we expect revenues of around $100 million. Then over the next several years, if the contracts we have in place continue to grow, there's no reason we won't grow to a quarter billion dollars annually within the next three years.

Now Nina Vaca and Pinnacle are reaping the rewards of their amazing rise from the ashes. The company has been named Minority Business Company of the Year by several national organizations. In 2003, Pinnacle was selected Hispanic Business Company of the Year by the Women's Business Council—Southwest and the 2003 Hispanic-Owned Business of the Year. Last year it ranked 78 among the nation's 500 fastest-growing privately held companies in the United States. Approximately 114,000 firms across all industries applied for the award.

Nina has twice been the recipient of the U.S. Hispanic Chamber of Commerce's prestigious Hispanic Businesswoman of the Year award. *Fast Company* selected her as one the top 25 women business builders in the country. She was also recently selected as one of the 50 most important Hispanics in business and technology by *Hispanic Engineering and Technology*. Most recently, she joined such visionaries as Dell Computer's Michael Dell and Starbuck's Howard Schultz in receiving the coveted Ernst & Young Entrepreneur of the Year award for technology and communications for the southwest region.

It's not just that Nina Vaca has built such a prestigious company, or that she has done it so quickly, but what is so inspirational is that she came back from the brink of oblivion when so many of the entrepreneurs around her were giving up and getting out. Hers is a triumph of the spirit. She embodies the idea that where there is a will, there will always be a way.

Whereas Bob Lorsch and Nina Vaca survived megadisasters many times, especially for small companies just starting out, a very small problem can almost bring a company to its knees. In the case of Steve Leveen's Levenger, Inc., it was a light switch. Leveen says:

One of the challenges we faced early on was unexpected, as most challenges are. The problem was a manufacturing defect and suppliers who were being less than truthful in owning up to those defects. In our case, we were selling these lamps to customers and the dimmer switches were failing on them. It was very expensive to ship the lamps back and forth, but it was lucky if the lamp made one trip to the customer, without being damaged, let alone to come back to us and then go back to the customer.

We made the decision early on, no matter what, that our customers would not suffer. So we refunded the money to our customers, and took care of all the shipping expenses and, as long as their patience held out, we would continue to send them products until they got a good one. Sometimes we had to send them three lamps. All the while, the manufacturer was telling us that we were the only ones with this problem, which we found out was not true. In the meantime, we lost a lot of money and spent a lot of time dealing with the issue.

Just as was true about learning from your mistakes, problems— even those that might seem insurmountable at the time—can teach invaluable lessons to the new entrepreneur. The light switch problem was a major lesson learned by Steve Leveen, and it might even be credited with teaching him a lesson about customer relations that has helped propel his company to the top. He says:

We didn't lose any customers over it as far as I know because we took care of them so well and told them the truth. One of the lessons for us was simply to always tell the truth to the customer. If you tell them the truth, they will forgive almost anything. That was an important lesson for us. Customers are much more important than any single sale. You should be willing to lose money on any sale in order to retain the customer. But this incident certainly put our service ethic to the test, right in our early days, and almost put us under. Finally, we just had to exit that manufacturer, who subsequently went out of business not surprisingly.

Sometimes, the disaster a business faces is that it has a better idea, but not enough people are ready to listen. Economists use the fancy term *market timing* for this, but it boils down to you simply being too early. Alex Pitt knows how that can happen, and what an entrepreneur has to do to recover from such a dilemma.

Alex represents many first-generation immigrants who come to the United States, see incredible opportunity, and then act on it. Born in the Ukraine, the son of a high-ranking government official, he comes from a family of scientists and mathematicians. He calls himself the first entrepreneur in his family.

Pitt is president of the National Merchant Center (NMC), an innovative company that helps businesses, both big and small, utilize technology to help grow their businesses. "The company started in 1996," Pitt explained to me. "We started originally installing e-payment solutions for Internet businesses. We were not successful because we were too early. There were not enough people using the Internet, accessing web sites, and making purchases."

Essentially, this new company, which had started with such high hopes, was dead in the water.

"We didn't fail; we were just ahead of our time," Pitt says. "No one could accuse us of being a failure because we were there at the beginning of an industry. We switched to retail operations so that we could be in compliance with new rules from the credit card issuers—Visa and MasterCard. We developed a number of innovative products to be sold differently from those being offered by other companies. My father was an engineer and I guess he taught me to think about building things new. From the first day of our business, our goal was to specialize in products and services to benefit customers, create something new, and then offer them at a cheaper, better price."

National Merchant Center is now an industry leader doing somewhere between $2 billion and $3 billion a year in electronic credit card processing, and they are on a path right now to double or triple that within the next year.

How do you survive whatever pothole you will be facing down the road? Fred Ruiz remembers the days well before his Mexican-style food company was very successful. He remembers overcoming the difficulties he faced:

> In business, you do have low points where it's difficult to see the light at the end of the tunnel. I can remember when my dad first started our business, the first five years was hand to mouth. We got to the point where I sat down and, doing the books, saw all the money that we owed to our vendors, looked at the amount of money that was coming in, and I said, "It looks like we have about two weeks left and then we're going to have to close the doors." My dad's response was, "Well, I guess we'll have to work a little harder."
>
> What he actually meant was not that we have to work a little harder, but rather we have to work a little smarter. We looked around at the marketplace, and we came up with a new product—tamales. We took the product to a lot of smaller retailers, mom-and-pop kinds of operations, and the timing was just perfect. It turned out to be an instant success.

This got us over the hump, and we were able to weather our financial difficulties. We learned a lot from this experience, about how to market new products and to take advantage of some of the changing facets of society such as women working outside the house and needing ways to quickly and easily fix dinner when they got home.

The bottom line is: We were able to work smarter, and that was a really important lesson to learn. It was an important lesson because, truthfully, I thought we were done.

There was another time we had a financial crisis because we had a loan with an insurance company that was called in because the insurance company decided it no longer wanted to loan money to businesses in the food industry. In a business like ours, you are always on the edge, and so something like this had to be seen as a crisis. We were able to overcome it, found another loan source, and in doing so we learned another lesson: Sometimes you can get too far out on the edge, and then you get caught. At times, we were in a position like this, but we managed to work our way through it.

If you're visiting Hawaii and staying in one of the many posh hotels, the chances are good that the croissant you had for breakfast, the French bread on the dinner table, or the wonderful French pastry you had for dessert came from 1 of the 24 bakery and sandwich shops around the Islands owned by one of my all-time favorite entrepreneurs, Thanh Quoc Lam, the SBA's Small Business Person of the Year in 2002.

No entrepreneur that I know has suffered the level of adversity only to survive and prosper than has Thanh. He literally started with nothing—the shirt on his back—and has ended up owning the multimillion-dollar Ba-Le Bakery chain that stretches from Hawaii to Japan and soon to China. Thanh explains:

I left Vietnam by boat (they called us the "boat people") in 1979. I arrived in California—San Jose—in September and for the first four months I was there, I was on welfare. I didn't speak any English, so I went to classes to learn. I went to work for the Intel Corporation, but I noticed that every one that was at work wore glasses. So I asked them if they had worn glasses before they started working and many said no. I noticed when I got home at night that I had headaches from working all day making the chip wafers. I didn't want my eyesight to go bad, so I quit.

After that, I held a number of jobs in gas stations, car washes, as a busboy, and as a house cleaner. But then, about a year after I had arrived in San Jose, I started my own business taking tourists to Reno, Nevada. I was paid by the casinos that gave me a commission on the number of tourists I would bring to their places. I did that for about four years and was making good money when a friend asked if I wanted to go into partnership with him in a sandwich shop in Hawaii. At the time, there was no one making Vietnamese sandwiches in Hawaii, and there was clearly a market for it.

Thanh and his friend Le Vo went to Hawaii and leased a grocery store in the Chinatown area of Honolulu. In 1984, the first Ba-Le sandwich shop opened. It was such an instant success that local suppliers could not keep up with the demand for fresh-baked French bread. In 1986, Thanh opened a second Ba-Le shop and bought out Le Vo's interest in the business, becoming the sole owner of Ba-Le. The interest on the loan he used to buy out his partner was crushing, so Thanh secured a direct loan from the SBA to pay off the original lender and to buy new and better equipment. Thanh now says with a laugh:

> When I started this, many in my family worried because I had never been in the food business before. But I told them I could learn, and in the beginning I did everything—cashier, cook, and clean up. The first couple of years, A to Z, the owner did it. I told my mother not to worry; if business was good, I could hire people; if it was slow, I could do everything myself and we would not lose money because the overhead was very low. For 25 years now, I've worked 90 to 100 hours a week.

It has paid off. Thanh recently told me, "Today sales are over $10 million annually. We have 24 locations, some of which are franchised to former employees. We now have about 110 employees."

Thanh is always looking for growth opportunities. Currently, he's expanding his sandwich and bakery business to Japan and China. He says:

> I never felt that I wouldn't make it and I never felt like quitting. There are many times when I got very tired. When I did, I thought back to what I had when I first came to America, and what I have now, and it gave me the incentive to push forward.
>
> I think I'm a success because of my good employees and because of my family. Fifty percent of my success is because of my employees, 30 percent is the effort of my wife and family, and maybe 20 percent is my hard work.

Mercedes LaPorta, while growing her electrical supply company often hit bumps in the road, but she learned early to keep moving forward.

"In this business, your suppliers have to be paid on a 30-day basis, but often if you get your money from a general contractor or building owner in 75 days, that's considered *great*," she explained. "A lot of times we wondered where we were going to get the money, worrying how we're going to make ends meet. There were a lot of sleepless nights. But in all 28 years, I've never considered there was anything I wouldn't be able to overcome, whatever problems I had at the time. I always knew I would find a way to do it, and I always did find a way to overcome the obstacles that were in my way.

These are examples of men and women who, even though they were dealt a harsh blow, were able to fight through their despair, overcome it, and then not only survive but thrive. All illustrate that it's not a question of *if* something bad or negative will happen to you or your business, but only a question of *when*.

The most important thing is what you do to move forward. It's not what happens to you, but what you make it mean that makes all the difference. We can't control everything that happens in our life, but we can control what we do and think about it. We are stronger than we know, and often, during the most difficult times, we are able to do miraculous, incredible things.

III

The Tools for Success

9

Where to Get the Critical Answers and Help

Let's review for a moment. From the experts we've talked with, and from the successful entrepreneurs who have given us their secrets, we've learned that the starting point for the new entrepreneur is to realize what he or she does not know. Then, even before starting a business, a certain amount of planning needs to be done.

We've learned that the most successful entrepreneurs do not fear making mistakes because they often consider mistakes to be invaluable for the lessons they teach. We've learned that a new business can often get a leg up by finding a niche that needs to be filled and then by crafting a business around filling that need.

We've seen that small business owners must be willing to take risks and must be ready to accept change. They must always realize that disasters, both big and small, often loom, but they can be weathered and companies can bounce back stronger than ever.

We've seen the importance of hiring the right people and the importance, especially as the business grows, of delegating responsibility to your employees. Finally, we've seen that challenging the conventional wisdom can often lead to success.

Many new small business owners will look at this list and the first thought that will come to mind is: "Where can a person turn to get help, especially if the budget won't support the hiring of a consultant or some other kind of outside expert?" This chapter offers some key suggestions in answer to this question.

Now, for a moment, let's turn back to some conventional wisdom. The conventional wisdom holds, "You always get what you pay for." The conventional wisdom also holds that if something seems "too good to be true," it usually is. Both of these thoughts are generally true, but I know of one situation where neither is true, and any smart small business owner or fledgling entrepreneur can get something invaluable for nothing by meeting with a SCORE counselor. You should jump at the opportunity.

Say you are thinking about starting a mail-order business. You don't know much about it, except you think you have a product that will lend itself to mail-order sales. You look around the mail-order marketplace and, perhaps because it is a mail-order company you personally have bought from, you think that someday you want to grow your company to be just like it.

You might think, "Boy, what wouldn't I give to sit down with the founder of Omaha Steaks and pick his brain about how I can get started in the mail-order business, and maybe convince him to help me. Wouldn't that be great?"

Is it a pipe dream to have one of the most successful mail-order marketers in the country counsel you? Not necessarily. What if I told you that one of the founders would be happy to sit down with you, or communicate with you via e-mail, and that it would cost you absolutely nothing—nada, be completely free and come with no strings attached?

Or let's say you are thinking about buying a floundering small business because you think it is a prime turnaround candidate that is available for a very attractive price. You might want to get a bit of help and advice on how to turn a business around. You could go to one of the big accounting or consulting firms and for a tidy fee they would give you that kind of advice. But what if I told you that John Carden, the retired vice chair of Ernst & Young, with 30 years of experience in strategic planning and turnaround assistance, is available to give you advice and his advice would be absolutely free?

Would this sound too good to be true? Well, I know where a small business owner, or a young entrepreneur contemplating starting a small business can get the best available one-on-one counseling and it will cost nothing. Because they counsel tens of thousands of small business owners every year, the organization is certainly not a secret, but many who are contemplating starting a small business don't automatically think of SCORE as a first stop. So, let me introduce you to SCORE.

SCORE

Throughout this book, we have seen some of the work of SCORE and its counselors. Since 1964, SCORE has provided free one-on-one counseling, in person and over the Internet, and has put on thousands of low-cost business workshops. The key word in that sentence is *free*.

SCORE-Counselors to America's Small Business is a nonprofit association dedicated to entrepreneur education and the formation, growth, and success of small business nationwide. SCORE is a resource partner with the U.S. Small Business Administration (SBA), which provides about half its funding. SCORE provides a public service to the United States by offering small business advice and training.

By the early 1960s, there were perhaps 50 or more independent groups across the country that were providing low-cost or no-cost business counseling. So on October 5, 1964, one of my predecessors, SBA Administrator Eugene P. Foley, officially launched SCORE—then called the Service Corps of Retired Executives—as a national volunteer group with 2,000 members, uniting independent efforts into a national force.

Since then, SCORE has helped more than 7.5 million small businesses, including many who have become household names. It offers face-to-face small business counseling at 389 chapter offices nationwide. Last year, SCORE recorded more than 423,000 total services that include face-to-face counseling, workshops, and online advice. There were 182,324 new counseling cases and 114,415 follow-up counseling sessions. No matter where you are, there is a SCORE chapter nearby. SCORE's volunteer counselors possess more than 600 business skills, and they speak many languages.

"The product that we offer is experience," explains Ken Yancey, SCORE's immensely talented and dedicated chief executive officer, who I had the great pleasure of working closely with in my years at the SBA.

"I have 11,000 volunteers who on average have a 30-year career in whatever industry or discipline they have been active in. So there is 300,000 years of business experience that is resident in the 11,000 members. Of that number, 20 to 25 percent are still employed. They're active and in business today so that the advice being given is current and never stale.

"We always do our best work in a mentoring relationship. In the longer-term relationship, we can better understand a business and the unique issues it faces, whatever unique challenges there are. We can help someone over time and can be a much better resource as opposed to somebody coming in looking for a transactional relationship—someone who comes in, asks a question, and leaves. Certainly, we can do a transaction—you want to know where to go to register your business, or have a question about hiring, or filing what form where. We will talk to you about that and give you the answer you're looking for, but we work much better in a longer-term relationship."

Many people who are just at the point of thinking about starting a business, or even earlier decided that being in business is right for them, might hesitate about going into SCORE, thinking they are not ready for the kind of counseling that SCORE offers. That is not true, says Yancey.

"I think that's a great time to come to SCORE. One of the unique things about us is that you can come to SCORE and simply ask the question: 'I've always wanted to have my own business, what do you think I ought to do?'

"We can talk to you about what your skills and abilities are, what your interests are, and what your hobbies are—where your strengths and weaknesses are and how you look at businesses that are suited to your abilities, talents, and interests. If you walk in and say you've always wanted to be an engineering consultant, but you're not an engineer, we will steer you elsewhere. But if you really love baseball cards, comic books, and other collectibles, there's likely a business in there somewhere and we will work with you to develop it. We can help you pull an idea out of your interests and assess whether there is a potential business, assuming there is a market for whatever it is you want to do. We can help you judge whether you have the capacity, if there is the market demand for it, and how you should possibly proceed."

Lou Campanelli of Port Washington, New York, had a long and distinguished career in the supermarket industry. He is now the national director for strategic alliances for SCORE and is also a long-time SCORE counselor to New York area entrepreneurs and is an advisor to the SCORE Association on alliance and development planning. He says that one of the strengths of SCORE is the ability of counselors to deter some potential business owners from making rash decisions, or from jumping into things before they are ready:

> If you come in looking to start a specific business, you should have some knowledge of that business. Everybody wants to open up a restaurant, but they don't know the first thing about it. They know when they go to a restaurant and they walk in, a person shakes their hand and it looks glamorous. But there's a lot more to opening a restaurant than that.

At times, people are just not ready to start a business.

"A man came in and said he wanted to go into the dog grooming business. But when we asked him, he admitted he did not know the first thing about dog grooming. So we told him he needed to go out and work for a dog groomer and learn the business. That was about six months ago and he did. Now he's come back with knowledge of the business and we're talking. We're working to get him started on his own."

How things ought to work, says Campanelli, thinking about some of his biggest successes as a counselor, is the story of Winston Torres.

"He first came in when he was fixing cars in his mother's backyard and garage. As of right now, five years later, he owns his own repair shop—Supreme Auto Repair in Port Washington, New York. He owns his own building, he has bought a house, and he's married with a child. He's gotten all this from repairing automobiles and the fact he does very good work at a fair price. He's just a very knowledgeable, hard-working young man."

Torres came into SCORE knowing he wanted to go into the auto repair business, but not much else.

"We helped him set up a line of credit and develop a business plan; we gave him advice on where to locate, helped him develop local advertising, and perhaps most important we got him certified to do government work so he is able to repair police cars and fire vehicles."

Almost all 389 SCORE chapters have counselors with the basics covered, but if you go in seeking answers to highly technical questions or looking for advice on starting a highly specialized business, the local chapter can look across the country for volunteers with the specialized knowledge you seek.

"No matter what your question is and what potential business you want to set up, it's not uncommon that we will have expertise within the specific chapter for what you need answered," says Yancey. "If we don't, we have the online counseling capability where we can match you up with any of our counselors nationally who has the specific knowledge you need.

"Today, online counseling represents about a third of the counseling we do. So you can go online and use keywords to search through a list of almost 2,000 volunteers to find a specific skill, ability, and depth of knowledge you're looking for. You can put in the keywords you're looking for, and we supply you a list of those counselors with the skill set who might be available to you. You can choose counselors based on a skills list in their bios and you can e-mail them directly and begin a mentoring relationship."

SCORE's strength and excellence is in one-on-one counseling, whether face-to-face or over the Internet, but it also puts on a wide range of small session seminars, either live or on the Web.

"SCORE offers somewhere in the neighborhood of 7,000 workshops annually," says Yancey. "They're on a variety of topics that relate to starting, managing, growing, buying, or selling a business. The seminars are driven at the local level and the chapter determines what the schedules are, what the topics are, and to an extent, the content. When you get in touch with your local chapter, they'll work with you to determine the best place for you. It's a great opportunity to learn in a group environment where you can bounce things off other people, learn from others, and you can network."

To find the SCORE office nearest you, log onto *http://www .score.org/findscore/chapter_maps.html*.

SMALL BUSINESS DEVELOPMENT CENTER NETWORK

If you are a small business owner or are thinking about starting a business, no matter where you live in the country, the chances are excellent that an academic institution nearby is able to offer you both classes and perhaps one-on-one counseling. The more than 1,000 Small Business Development Center (SBDC) network service centers are hosted by universities, community colleges, and state economic development agencies in all 50 states. Funded by Congress as part of the SBA's annual budget, they exist to provide business owners, or perspective business owners, with no-cost consulting and fee-charging training. Small business owners and aspiring entrepreneurs can go to their local SBDCs for free consulting and at-cost training in subjects like writing business plans, obtaining capital, marketing, regulatory compliance, international trade, and the like.

The SBDCs were established by Congress in 1980 as a public-private partnership that includes Congress, the SBA, major private sector companies, universities, community colleges, and state governments that manage the local SBDCs across the nation. Congress, through the SBA, provides approximately $100 million a year in funding that each local SBDC must match dollar for dollar from local fund-raising through corporate sponsorship and the value of in-kind services provided by the host institutions.

The local SBDC offices serve over 700,000 clients annually and offer entrepreneurial education through outreach and education including individual counseling, training, and research assistance.

One of the nation's most outstanding SBDCs is the Southwest Texas Border Region Small Business Development Center based at the University of Texas, San Antonio (UTSA). Robert M. McKinley is the regional director and associate vice president for economic development of the UTSA Institute for Economic Development. He says:

> Small Business Development Centers are a partnership program between the U.S. Small Business Administration and the higher education institutions in the United States. It started many years ago as a pilot program to provide management technical assistance to small businesses. Over time, it's grown and evolved to become market-driven to respond to the needs of the small business community and to respond to the economic climate.
>
> A particular value of having the SBDCs aligned with higher education is that higher education is traditionally invested in research and, with business today evolving, you need a translator between the scientist and the business community. The SBDCs being extension agents of the colleges are perfectly situated to the task, whether it is working with the Small Business Innovation Research (SBIR) program, getting venture capital, doing the commercialization activities, performing research, or helping with intellectual property.
>
> Almost all SBDCs have valuable materials available on the Internet. For instance, here at the University of Texas, San Antonio, we have the national SBDC Clearinghouse. We have researchers, economists, and graduate students so that any SBDC in the country that has a research request—such as a market study or intellectual property search—can access that information via a request. We have it back to the counselor in time for his next appointment. We've completed over 30,000 of those requests.

You can find the SBDC nearest you by logging onto: *http://www.sba.gov /localresources/* or *http://www.sba.gov/aboutsba/sbaprograms /sbdc/sbdclocator/index.html*; and you can log onto the web site of the SBDC National Information Clearinghouse at *http://sbdcnet.org/* and find a wealth of information that you can view and download.

PROCUREMENT TECHNICAL ASSISTANCE CENTER

If you want to sell to the federal government, one of your first stops should be your nearest Procurement Technical Assistance Center (PTAC—pronounced "Pee-Tack"), with over 250 local offices around the country.

Each PTAC has experienced counselors who meet with small business owners to explain all the fine points of government contracting. Visit *http://www.aptac-us.org* for basic information and the location of the PTAC nearest you.

U.S. EXPORT ASSISTANCE CENTERS

These centers are located in major metropolitan areas throughout the United States. They are one-stop shops ready to provide a small- or medium-sized business with local export assistance. You can receive personalized assistance from professionals in the U.S. Small Business Administration, the U.S. Department of Commerce, the U.S. Export-Import Bank, and other public and private organizations. Visit *http://www.sba.gov/aboutsba/sbaprograms /internationaltrade/useac/index.html.*

KAUFFMAN CENTER FOR ENTREPRENEURIAL LEADERSHIP

Ewing Marion Kauffman was an amazing story of entrepreneurial success. From Kansas City, Missouri, he started working as a pharmaceutical salesman after World War II. In 1950, he started his own pharmaceutical company in the basement of his home. When he sold his company to Merrell Dow in 1989, it had grown to become an international giant with nearly $1 billion in sales and 3,400 employees.

He owned the Kansas City Royals and was a civic leader. He established the Ewing Marion Kauffman Foundation in the mid-1960s to help young people, especially those from disadvantaged backgrounds, get a quality education that would enable them to reach their full potential. He saw building enterprise as one of the most effective ways to realize individual promise and spur the economy. The Kauffman Foundation has grown into the 26th largest foundation in the United States with an asset base of approximately $2 billion and today is dedicated to education and entrepreneurship. It spends about $90 million of endowment income per year on grants, programs, and related expenses.

The Kauffman Foundation is the only large U.S. foundation to focus on entrepreneurship. The Foundation is a center for research, sponsors educational initiatives at the college level, gives scholarships, and has a huge searchable database of research, white papers, and how-to guides that are assessable by anyone owning a small business, growing business, or thinking about starting a small business.

Carl Schramm is president and chief executive officer of the Ewing Marion Kauffman Foundation. Above all, Schramm is an optimist about entrepreneurship. He is also a glass half-full kind of person. While I remain appalled at the failure rates among new start-up businesses, he thinks there is a positive side to the numbers.

"I think it's important not to look at the failure rate of these businesses but rather at the success rate. If a few years ago 50 percent of small businesses were said to be succeeding after five years, and today it's four years, that's an improvement. The real issue is not how many fail, but how many survive."

The Foundation is a vital source of information not only for academics but also for everyday small business owners. To access the Foundation's vast database, log onto *http://www.eventuring .org/eShip/appmanager/eVenturing/eVenturingDesktop.*

WOMEN-OWNED BUSINESSES

Today, in the United States women own 50 percent or more of 10.4 million business firms. These firms employ more than 12.8 million people and generate $1.9 trillion in annual sales. For the past two decades, these firms have continued to grow at almost two times the rate of all firms.

One of the most passionate women entrepreneurs I know is my former deputy administrator at the SBA, Melanie Sabelhaus. She remembers:

> When I came to the SBA, I set out to work on issues important to women entrepreneurs. The first was healthcare. In my company, I wanted to be able to offer my employees healthcare benefits. I would lose sleep at night over the issue because of the costs involved. Something had to be done.
>
> Then, too, there was the issue of access to financing. I had been turned down 13 times before I got my initial financing and access to

capital was critical to me to allow me to grow my company and to become what it became. Without that financing, I could never have lived up to my potential.

I didn't know that the SBA provided assistance at over 1,200 Small Business Development Centers around the country; and I didn't know that there were over 100 Women's business centers where a woman could walk in and sit down with a counselor, take classes, and explore the possibilities of starting her own business and living her dream. I didn't know we had SCORE counselors across the country, experienced business executives who will sit down with you and work with you on establishing or marketing your business. Opening the door for women became my goal.

At the SBA, Melanie and I devoted a great deal of energy to ensuring that women-owned businesses were integrated into everything the SBA did. The SBA developed www.womenbiz.gov, a web site to assist women business owners in accessing the federal marketplace. This site provides links to over 100 procurement web sites, including links to all of the major federal agencies. It also includes a section on how to get started in this invaluable business arena.

There is a great deal of additional help and information readily available for the women entrepreneurs both supplied by the federal government and the quasi-private sector—usually by not-for-profit organizations dedicated to women business owners.

Other great resources include:

Women-21—http://women-21.gov

The federal government's one-stop resource for women entrepreneurs operated by the U.S. Department of Labor and the SBA. It is a wide-ranging repository of targeted information, registration for online programs, and networking opportunities to help women business owners or women considering opening businesses. It also contains a valuable small business tools and tips section.

National Women's Business Council (NWBC)— http://www.womenbiz.gov; www.nwbc.gov

A bipartisan federal advisory council created by Congress as part of the Women's Ownership Act of 1988 to serve as an independent source of advice and policy recommendations to the president, Congress, and the SBA on economic issues of importance to women business owners. Members of NWBC are prominent women business owners and leaders of women's business organizations.

The NWBC conducts research on issues of importance to women business owners and their organizations and connects the members of the women's business community to one another and to public policymakers.

National Association of Women Business Owners (NAWBO)—http://www.nawbo.org

A national dues-based organization representing the interests of all women entrepreneurs across all industries. Since 1975, NAWBO has helped women in business by sharing resources and providing a single voice to shape economic and public policy. Today, the organization features chapters in almost every metropolitan area in the United States. Membership is open to sole proprietors, partners, and corporate owners with day-to-day management responsibility. Active members who live in a chapter area automatically join both their local chapter and national. Members can access a variety of opportunities, products, and services that will help their businesses achieve greater visibility, credibility, and profitability.

Association of Women's Business Centers (AWBC)— http://www.awbc.biz

A national not-for-profit organization representing women's business centers and women business owners. Founded in 1998, AWBC supports entrepreneurial development among women through education, training, mentoring, business development, and financing opportunities. The organization provides information exchange, education, and training opportunities for women business centers and women-owned businesses.

Women's Business Enterprise National Council (WBENC)—http://www.wbenc.org

Founded in 1997, WBENC is the nation's leading advocate of women-owned businesses as suppliers to U.S. corporations.

It also is the largest third-party certifier of businesses owned and operated by women in the United States. The WBENC is a resource for the more than 700 U.S. companies and government agencies that rely on WBENC certification as an integral part of their supplier diversity programs.

eWomenNetwork, Inc.—http://www.ewomennetwork.com
Dallas-based, this is the fastest growing membership-based professional women's networking organization in North America. Through "Accelerated Networking" events, workshops and conferences, personal one-on-one executive coaching, and networking, women connect and network with each other in a secure Internet environment.

Center for Women's Business Research—
http://www. womensbusinessresearch.org
A source on the trends, characteristics, achievements, and challenges of women business owners and their enterprises.

MINORITY-OWNED BUSINESSES

There are also resources available to minorities who own or want to start their own businesses, including:

Minority Business Development Agency (MBDA)—
http://www.mbda.gov
A part of the U.S. Department of Commerce, MBDA is the only federal agency created specifically to foster the establishment and growth of minority-owned businesses in the United States. MBDA provides funding for a network of Minority Business Development Centers (MBDCs), Native American Business Development Centers (NABDCs), and Business Resource Centers (BRCs) located throughout the nation. The Centers provide minority entrepreneurs with one-on-one assistance in writing business plans, marketing, management and technical assistance, and financial planning to assure adequate financing for business ventures. The Centers are staffed by business specialists who have the knowledge and practical experience needed to run successful and profitable

businesses. Their web site provides access to the local programs plus other in-depth information.

VETERAN-OWNED BUSINESSES

There are considerable resources available to veterans who own or want to start their own businesses including:

U.S. Small Business Administration's Office of Veterans Business Development (OVBD)— http: //www.sba.gov/vets

Dedicated to serving the veteran entrepreneur by formulating, executing, and promoting policies and programs of the agency that provide assistance to veterans seeking to start and develop small businesses. Links are provided to OVBD officers in the SBA's district offices who can help veterans prepare to start businesses and to the Veterans Business Outreach Program (VBOP), which is designed to provide entrepreneurial development services such as business training, counseling, and mentoring to eligible veterans owning or considering starting a small business.

Veterans Affairs Business Programs for Veterans— http://www1.va.gov/opa/fact/ventfs.html

A subdivision of the Office of Small and Disadvantaged Business Utilization, this organization was created to make it easier for veterans to establish and expand their businesses. The Center was established by the Veterans Entrepreneurship and Small Business Development Act of 1999 and was officially dedicated on February 14, 2001. The Center's mission is to promote veterans' business enterprises.

Center for Veterans' Enterprise—http://www.vetbiz.gov

The Veteran Resource Information web site was designed to assist veteran entrepreneurs who want to start and expand their businesses in the federal and private marketplace. It includes access to being listed on a veteran database that lists businesses that are 51 percent or more owned by veterans or service-connected disabled veterans and that is used to promote and market veteran-owned small businesses (VOSBs) and service-disabled veteran-owned small businesses (SDVOSBs). This database is the number one source for federal agencies looking for SDVOSBs. It connects to an electronic clearinghouse that provides a wealth of resources for the veteran contemplating small business ownership and veteran small business owners considering expansion. It also provides business coaching, networking, and outreach from in-house experts to help veteran business owners with specific business questions, brainstorming, and counseling.

State Veterans Business Development Centers— http://www.sba.gov/gopher/Business-Development /Veterans Affairs/Veterans-Locations

Each state has an office to help local veteran-owned businesses, particularly to do business with the state. This web site provides access to the offices in all 50 states.

Disabled Veterans Business Enterprise (DVBE) Network— http://www.elitedvbe.org/dvbemambo/index.php

An organization comprised of certified DVBEs whose purpose is to provide a forum where members meet to discuss the benefits of membership.

Veterans Corporation—http://www.Veteranscorp.org

The National Veterans Business Development Corporation (the Veterans Corporation) is a federally chartered organization charged with creating and enhancing entrepreneurial business opportunities for veterans, including service-disabled veterans. Provides veterans with the tools and resources they need to be successful in business including access to capital, access to business services, entrepreneurial education, surety bonding, insurance, and a veterans' business directory.

Boots2Business—www.boots2business.com

A program of the Veterans Corporation presents the leading on-line resources in education and workplace training, uniquely tailored to meet the needs of military personnel, including Guard and Reserve, Veterans, Service-Disabled Veterans, and their families. The elements comprising Boots2Business have been successfully used independently and the Veterans Corporation has integrated them into a cohesive and interactive online program.

MENTORS

It should not be an embarrassment to not know something or to be struggling. It's much worse to plow through a business plan that isn't working without seeking help. It's much more of a failure not to seek help, than to ask for it. The good news is there are plenty of people out there who know the answers you need and who are more than willing to come to your aid if you just realize you need those answers and need that help—before it is too late.

We've just discussed some of the organizational help that is available to you. Your best source is SCORE, but there is another way to go, one that is more direct, but it is a bit more difficult because the legwork is up to you. Find a guardian angel—not a financial angel, although those are always helpful—that is, someone who understands what you are going through and who will help watch over you. You need to find a *mentor*.

Fred Ruiz, head of Mexican food giant Ruiz Foods, says he would not be where he is today without the help of others.

"I've never been afraid to ask for help. I would hear about a company that was having the same kinds of problems that I was, but had managed to overcome them, and I would call the owner of the company, introduce myself, and ask how he had managed to overcome these difficulties. What I learned was that people, especially successful people, are very willing to help you and want to help. If they have the time, they give you great advice. I can't tell you how many times I have done this and how willing people are to share from their experience."

Steve Leveen, owner of high-end retailer Levenger, Inc., agrees.

"There's an old adage, 'When the student is ready, the teacher appears.' Businesspeople, especially those just starting out, must be open to learning from others. It's been my experience that there are plenty of people out there with relevant experience who are ready to help. Some of them have the time and the experience to be a mentor, of passing on their knowledge, wisdom, and techniques. When I give talks to business students occasionally, I tell them to go out and find their Obi-Wan Kenobi, or maybe it should be their Yoda, because, sometimes like Yoda, they will come in unexpected packages. They may be old and wizened; they may be your contemporary; who knows what they're going to look like."

Mitchell Rubinson, a Miami-based serial entrepreneur, also believes mentors are an invaluable asset and ally for any new small business owner.

"One of the first things young entrepreneurs should do is to try to find a mentor," he says. "That should actually be fairly simple to do. Every successful businessperson, at least most successful businesspeople, are happy to help a young person coming up. They are honored by your asking. They will give you honest advice. If you select properly, and you've done your research, you can use them as a sounding board and the beauty of it is they have no jealousy."

But he also has a warning about who you should look to as possible mentors. He warns that you should exclude your peers.

"They want to see you succeed," he says referring to successful people you might approach. "The more you win the better they feel, because they feel that they are a part of your success; whereas, if you deal with one of your contemporaries, there can be all kinds of jealousy and competitive aspects. It's great if you have old friends, but don't involve them in a business situation because just by your friendship you're all equals. They don't want to see you do more than them.

"You have to realize at the beginning, many of your peers simply don't want you to succeed. This will manifest itself in many ways. They all watch because if you win that makes you smarter than them."

Rebecca Matthias, who built Mothers Work Inc. from a small mail-order catalog business being run out of her bedroom into an international behemoth, remembers how important both mentors and role models were to her starting out:

> I had mentors, and I had role models. It was important to me to see other women who were successful and able to start and run a big business.

By looking at them, I knew that I could do that too. Looking at them was something that was an inspiration for me.

When I was just starting out, I remember I went to a seminar for women in business and Debbie Fields was the speaker—the lady who started Mrs. Fields cookies. At that time, she was a huge role model for me. I had read about her and listened to her tell her story about how she started with a little store and took a tray of cookies out into the parking lot and offered them to people in order to get feedback. Now she had this huge business, this $500 million business, and it just seemed to me that if she could do that, I could do it too.

But she makes a distinction between role models who can be valuable because they can inspire, and mentors who can be very hands-on and directly help you in your business:

I remember when I first started, I used to go to the library to check out books on inspiring stories of people who start businesses and their great successes, especially women. It was like this need I had to know that somebody else had done what I was trying to do. These people became my role models by example—they didn't have to be anyone I knew.

But then I was fortunate to get Verna Gibson on my board. She founded The Limited, and those were the days when it was growing. She had started small, and now it was getting large and I thought if she could do it, I could too. It was really helpful to me to have that role model and mentor.

It was important to have someone who could tell me, "I did this, or I did that," and how it worked out and "maybe you should try this or try that." That's a true mentor, like an advisor, someone who has a stake in what happens to you but isn't really running the show.

Rebecca Matthias was on to something when she had the foresight, and maybe the good luck, of adding a pioneering women entrepreneur and retailer to her board who was willing to share lessons learned and to point Rebecca in the right direction.

Another way to try to get this kind of hands-on help is to formulate a board of advisors. Jennifer Lawton, who we met earlier, founded and sold a technology company, became a senior executive at a larger technology company, and then got out of the technology business by buying a bookstore and coffee house. She utilized this technique to great advantage, writing about it for the Kaufman Foundation. In her essay, "If You Don't Know the Way, Just Ask Directions," Lawton details the process she and her partners took:

Many people think that you have to be a big company or an incorporated company to have a board of advisors or directors. Even a small company will benefit by having a board. Although my business was of modest size, I can't say enough about the value of its advisory board or board of directors.

When I started Net Daemons Associates (NDA) in 1991, I knew nothing about running a business. I knew a lot about technology, supporting computer networks, and using the Internet, but not much at all about sales, writing proposals, marketing material, invoicing, or collections—the basics of business. Seven years later, following a successful exit from the business through acquisition, I know enough about the business world to be a valuable director and advisory board member for other emerging growth companies.

For months, I carted around an article by Norm Brodsky on advisory boards, and finally I decided to recruit an advisory board for my company, following his plan to the letter. It was a long process, with a lot of formality, but well worth it. First my partners—Rudy Ventresca and Chris Caldwell—and I identified candidates, called them, and invited them to apply for membership on our board. We followed up with letters, personal interviews, and, finally, offers to join the board for a specified term. That ensured an escape hatch if the relationship didn't work out. By the end of the process, we were all very well aligned on joint expectations and were able to hit the road running at our first meeting.

Because we didn't know a lot about business, we seeded our board with members who had sales, marketing, finance, legal, operations, engineering, and technology backgrounds. NDA's first advisory board was composed of our mentors, people we already knew and trusted and who we felt were at a level of knowledge above our own at the time. Everyone on the board was known to one of us, the cofounders, who made up the management team. One advisor was a senior sales executive in high tech, another a marketing executive. We also recruited a banker, a lawyer, a senior engineering manager, and a venture capitalist.

As the company grew, the board membership changed, and eventually the advisory board became our board of directors. Every company needs directors—by definition, a corporation must have a board. At the very least, the board handles the legal and accounting issues that are required for overall governance. When we moved to a board of directors from an advisory board, the issues that we dealt with were increasingly focused around performance: keeping to an approved budget, and strategic and operational plans.

As we grew and continued to evolve and move up in the world, we added discussions about how to get bigger faster, what our exit strategy was, and how to execute that strategy. In the end, our board was heavily

involved, not just in voting to approve our acquisitions but also in determining what the structure, valuation, and due diligence process would be.

An important benefit of the board was keeping us honest. We didn't
necessarily have the ability to keep ourselves on schedule and on track to
update our strategic and operations plans, look forward to where we were
going, and ensure that we had proper financial management in place—but
the board did. Because of the board, we managers kept very current with
our planning and reporting and as a result were held accountable by someone other than ourselves.

She elaborated when I talked with her.

"You have to be up-front with advisors as to what you are
hoping to get from the relationship. Obviously, you also have to
guarantee that you will not be imposing or taking too much of
their time. In our case, it was a quarterly meeting and some were
willing to be more involved than that over time."

Then there is the flip side of all this. Once you have become a
success, possibly by getting help from one or more mentors, you
owe it to those who are coming along behind you, the next generation of entrepreneurs, to become a mentor and to help them.

Melanie Sabelhaus, my former deputy, is very passionate about
this—about the need for you to become a mentor:

> I learned to make sure to give back what I've gotten, and to mentor others
> once I had achieved a certain level. My greatest love is to be able to say,
> "Come with me, and let me show you the way. I've been there, I've done it.
> I've learned, and let me share with you the mistakes I've made because you
> are going to fail and you have to be able to pick yourself up and to start
> moving forward again. So pick yourself up, move on."
>
> To me, our next generation is going to be our greatest generation,
> and mentoring them is my contribution.

In our interviews, many have talked about the importance of
reaching out to others and asking for help. But don't be disappointed or discouraged if the first time you ask for help, someone
is busy, going through a bad time personally, or maybe just having
a lousy day. Keep asking. Let them know you admire them, respect
their time, and would like to learn from them. Most successful
people will appreciate that and want to give back and expect you
to someday give back to those who come behind you.

I remember as kids, my sisters and I would tell our parents that someday, we would pay them back for all that they gave us. But my parents, ever the wise teachers they were, would tell us that there is no way we would be able to pay them back. And they didn't expect us to pay them back, but what they did expect us to do is to pass it on to our children, and in that regard contribute to this wonderful cycle of life. None of us should abuse the generosity that we receive from other people in our lives. We should pass this generosity on.

10

Government and Big Business
Want to Help

For a number of years now, the federal government has worked hard to make more procurement opportunities available for small business. When I joined the Small Business Administration (SBA), one of the key goals in the president's small business agenda was providing access to procurement opportunities for small business.

Over time, this ideal of providing more opportunities for small business has become more difficult and challenging for government because less resources are allocated for procurement inside agencies and the entire procurement system has become more complex and, in recent years, Web-based.

Although only a limited number, relatively speaking, of small businesses seek contracts from the government, the small business community as a whole feels strongly on the subject and considers government contracting to be almost a litmus test of whether government is doing everything possible to provide opportunities for small businesses. It's almost like owners are thinking, "Even though I don't currently do business with the government, it doesn't mean that I might not want to do so in the future or that I don't want other small businesses to be able to participate in government contracting programs."

There is much passion around this issue, and I understand it; especially considering the contribution that small businesses make to the U.S. economy. Consider the fact that small business generates somewhere around 70 percent of the net new jobs in the economy. They represent over 50 percent of the private workforce, and they generate 52 percent of the gross domestic product of the economy, as well as most of the innovation that makes our economy the most productive economy in the world. In addition, they represent 97 percent of all businesses involved with international trade.

There is nothing small about small business when you consider those types of contributions. Is it any wonder that small business feels entitled to a fair share of the procurement opportunities?

There are 25 million small businesses in the United States. That is a huge market. You can't turn on the television or radio or read a newspaper without some mention of a small business. This is a market that cannot be ignored by large corporations or government.

DOING BUSINESS WITH THE GOVERNMENT

If you are a small business owner, the federal government not only *wants* to do business with you, by law it *must* use its best efforts to do business with you. The goal is that 23 percent of everything the government purchases, from paper clips to aircraft carrier's components, should come from small business.

Let me start by asking a seemingly obvious, yet critical question: What is the government's definition of a small business concern? This is critical, because to take advantage of the many federal programs designed for small business, your enterprise must qualify as a small business. Moreover, most major private corporations use the federal government's definitions to determine whether an enterprise they are doing business with is a small business.

People always ask me what defines a small business. The good news is most businesses in the United States fit the small business definition. The SBA is charged with defining what constitutes a small business. Overall, the SBA defines a small business concern as one that is independently owned and operated, is organized for profit, and is not dominant in its field. Depending on the industry, eligibility is based on the average number of employees for the preceding 12 months or on sales volume averaged over a three-year period.

The best place to go to find out whether your business qualifies is the SBA. You can call your local district office or you can go online to *http://www.sba.gov/services/contractingopportunities /sizestandardstopics/index.html* and get specific information on how businesses in your industry are defined.

The federal government requires that each of its agencies allocate a certain percentage of its contracts to small business. This policy, called the Government-Wide Procurement Preference Goaling Program, helps small businesses grow and create jobs and it stimulates the economy.

The federal government's statutory goal of 23 percent was achieved three years in a row during my tenure. That is the first time in history this was accomplished. In 2001, the federal government gave small business $50 billion in contracts. Four years later, the federal government gave $80 billion in contracts to small business. That is a 60 percent increase. Those are huge numbers, but it doesn't mean that government can rest on its laurels. Progress has been made, but there is still more that can be done to assist all types of small businesses in achieving their fair share of the federal procurement pie.

Note: The Small Business Act (Public Law 644 §15g) sets *"goals"* as opposed to absolute statutory *requirements.* The most misunderstood part of the law is that it requires only that the federal government and its various agencies must make a best effort to achieve various goals in buying from small business, not that it absolutely must give a specific percentage of its purchasing business to small business. Each must provide the maximum practicable opportunity to small businesses to win awards and must work to improve its procurement processes to meet the goals.

A number of federal agencies have exemplary records for buying from small businesses. The Department of Housing and Urban

Development, the Commerce Department, and the Defense Department are examples of agencies that consistently purchase from small businesses. A relatively new agency, the Department of Homeland Security (DHS) has implemented an effective program to ensure small business has wide-ranging procurement opportunities. That's quite a feat considering how young the agency is compared to government departments that have been a part of the federal bureaucracy for generations.

As mentioned earlier, Dan F. Sturdivant, assistant to the director of the DHS's Office of Small and Disadvantaged Business Utilization, is one of the deans of the government's small business initiative and one of the federal government's top procurement experts. As he explains the law and the regulations, "It means that I don't have to award you a specific contract; it only means that I have to ensure you have a level playing field on which to compete for that contract."

In describing how DHS's small business procurement operation works, Dan Sturdivant is really describing the government-wide effort.

"Like every other federal agency we have a responsibility," Sturdivant says. "We have an Office of Small and Disadvantaged Business Utilization, as does every federal agency that has the power to procure. Our responsibility is not to buy but rather oversight, internal and external training, reviewing to ensure the statutory goals given us by SBA are met, and making sure our small business specialists who are co-located at each of our buying units are cognizant of the program and how it works, and their responsibilities to the program as well."

Many large private sector organizations have lists of approved vendors they work from in buying from small businesses. You first have to qualify to get on their list before you can bid on contracts or before one of their procurement officers can send business your way. The federal government—except for certain agencies like the Transportation Security Administration, certain departments within the Department of Defense and the intelligence community, and when dealing with contracts that require prior security clearances—generally doesn't work that way.

"We don't have a qualification process, and we don't have a vendors list," says Sturdivant. Nor does the agency have any financial requirements of the small businesses they buy from. We assume that if they have been certified, they are ready to hit the ground running. We do have the Simplified Acquisition Program (SAP) that is on micropurchases of $2,500 and under all the way up to $100,000. All of these are set aside for small business. I call them "get your foot in the door" requirements. So you should find the SAP specialist to help you and you can start with these SAP requirements to get your foot in the door and then you start to build a relationship."

He is also able to add perspective to dealing with the federal government.

"Four things drive business: processes, relationships, homework, and niche versus need. Everything is process. If you don't know the process, and trust me there is one, you just have to discover it. There are relationships—people do business with people they know and they usually do business with people they like."

One advantage of trying to sell to agencies of the federal government is that they often know far in advance what their specific procurement needs will be based both on past purchases and on purchase contracts that are up for renewal.

Virtually every agency publishes a "Forecast of Contracting Opportunities of [the upcoming] Fiscal Year." It lists in great detail procurements that will be sought from the October 1 start of the new fiscal year. In addition, virtually every agency constantly updates this list whenever new opportunities become known, often well in advance. Go to the individual agency's web site and under the procurement section look for "Acquisition Forecast Database."

Many small business owners believe that the process of selling to the federal government is so complex and so filled with red tape that it simply is not worth the effort. But my experience in meeting with dozens and dozens of small business owners who are government contractors is they are—generally—very happy with the relationship, especially in the fact they never have to worry about getting paid. Once you get the hang of it, the federal government is very good to work with.

Use the following guidelines to approach doing businesses with the government:

- Target your market.
- Be competitive.
- Be persistent.
- Be patient.

SET-ASIDES

As mentioned, the federal government has a statutory goal that 23 percent of prime contracts should go to small businesses. Congress first enacted a procurement goal in prime contracting for small business in 1988. Since then, the goals have been increased and have been extended to include requirements that both agencies and so-called federal "prime contractors" must provide "maximum practicable opportunities in acquisitions" to certain specific categories of small business ownership: veteran-owned small business, service-disabled veteran-owned small business, historically underutilized business zone (HUBZone) small business, small disadvantaged business, and women-owned small business. There are specific statutory goals establishing set-asides for specific categories of small business owners. Currently, these goals are:

- 5 percent of prime and subcontracts for small disadvantaged businesses;
- 5 percent of prime and subcontracts for women-owned small businesses;
- 3 percent of prime contracts for HUBZone small businesses; and
- 3 percent of prime and subcontracts for service-disabled veteran-owned small businesses

So let's look at these specific programs.

Small Disadvantaged Businesses

The SBA administers two of the federal government's specific business assistance programs for small disadvantaged businesses (SDBs).

These programs are the 8(a) Business Development program and the Small Disadvantaged Business Certification Program. They are often confused or considered a single program, but they are different. The 8(a) program offers a broad scope of assistance to businesses owned by members of socially and economically disadvantaged groups. The SDB Certification Program is limited to offering benefits in federal procurement. Section 8(a) firms automatically qualify for SDB certification.

THE 8(a) BUSINESS DEVELOPMENT PROGRAM

Named for a section of the Small Business Act, the 8(a) program was created to help small disadvantaged businesses compete in the U.S. economy and access the federal procurement marketplace.

This is a program to help disadvantaged small businesses access procurement opportunities with the federal government. It is a business development program and can't guarantee a contract. It should provide access and a level playing field to companies that in the past were excluded or didn't have the same chance to participate through no fault of their own. Often, these small businesses are in the minority community.

Section 8(a) of the Small Business Act, authorizes the SBA to enter into contracts with procuring agencies and then to subcontract the actual performance to certain small business concerns. The original intention was to assure that small businesses would be efficiently utilized in war mobilization. However, under President Richard M. Nixon, the authority of the SBA was first used to assist small disadvantaged business firms.

To qualify for 8(a) status, an enterprise:

* Must be a small business,
* Must be unconditionally owned and controlled by one or more socially and economically disadvantaged individuals who are of good character and citizens of the United States, and
* Must demonstrate potential for success.

When I started at the SBA, there were approximately 6,000 firms that had 8(a) certification. That is a very small percentage considering that 15 percent of all businesses in the United States are considered minority businesses. That equates to approximately three million small businesses.

Of the 6,000 certified firms, only 3,000, or 50 percent, had ever received a government contract. About 200 firms received the majority of the contracts. Can you guess where those 200 firms were located? If you guessed near Washington, DC, you were correct. I considered the program to have become too top-heavy and it wasn't serving its original intent. So we dedicated ourselves to improving the distribution of contracts and to registering more firms in the program. When I left, we had increased the number of participating companies by 50 percent. It is still not enough, but it is certainly an improvement.

The Small Disadvantaged Businesses Program

Even if a company does not qualify for 8(a) status—often because it has not been in business for long enough—it can still qualify for designation as a SDB. Although SDB certification pertains only to federal contracting, it can be a significant benefit to a small business.

If a SDB-certified firm bids on a government contract, it receives a price evaluation adjustment of up to 10 percent on pro-curements—those usually over $100,000. This means that while the company will be paid its full bid price, when its offer is evaluated against those of competitors for the contract, it will be considered up to 10 percent less, giving the SDB a 10 percent advantage. The price evaluation adjustment does not apply to 8(a) acquisitions and small business set-asides.

You can obtain more information at: *http://www.sba.gov/sdb.*

Women-Owned Small Businesses

On June 22, 1983, President Ronald Reagan signed Executive Order 12138, which created the President's Advisory Committee on Women Business Ownership to focus the federal government's continuing interest in aiding women-owned small businesses. Women-owned small businesses are firms that are at least 51 percent owned, controlled, and operated by a woman or a group of women and whose management and daily business operations are controlled by women.

Each federal agency's Office of Small and Disadvantaged Business Utilization—and they all have one—identify women-owned small businesses and their capabilities. Each agency provides this information to its contracting offices and encourages them to issue solicitations and obtain proposals from qualified small firms. Participating agencies have designated women-owned business advocates to work with the SBA and women business owners to provide outreach, training, and marketing assistance.

Historically Underutilized Business Zones

Historically underutilized business zones (HUBZones) are part of the Small Business Reauthorization Act of 1997 in which Congress determined that in order to stimulate economic development and create jobs in economically depressed urban and rural communities, federal contracting preferences should be given to small businesses that maintain a "principal office"—but not necessarily a headquarters—in that zone and that 35 percent of their employees in this principal office live in one of these specially designated areas. Congress believed that fostering the growth of these businesses over the long term helps to empower communities, create jobs, and attract private investment to depressed areas.

Communities can apply to the SBA to have portions of their communities designated as HUBZones, and the agency, using census data, also designates such zones. It maintains a list of all zones and this list can be accessed via the SBA's web site.

To qualify for the program, a business must meet the SBA's small business standards and must be owned and controlled at least 51 percent by U.S. citizens, a Community Development Corporation, an agricultural cooperative, or an Indian tribe. An existing business can choose to move to a qualified area. To fulfill the requirement that 35 percent of a HUBZone firm's employees reside in the HUBZone, employees must live in a primary residence within that area for at least 180 days or be a currently registered voter in that area.

Service-Disabled Veteran-Owned Small Businesses

On December 16, 2003, Congress passed the Veterans Benefits Act of 2003. Section 308 of the law established a procurement program for service-disabled veteran-owned small business concerns (SDVOSBC). This procurement program provides that federal contracting officers may restrict competition to SDVOSBCs and award a sole source or set-aside contract where certain criteria are met. President George W. Bush then signed Executive Order 13360 on October 20, 2004, to significantly increase contracting opportunities for these individuals.

In January 2005, as the SBA administrator, I informed all federal agencies that under the president's executive order they must immediately develop a strategy to implement the policy, make the agency's strategy publicly available, and report annually to me on implementation of the agency's strategy and designate a senior-level official to be responsible for developing and implementing the agency's strategy. Included in the agency's strategy plan is the reserving of agency contracts exclusively for service-disabled veteran businesses, encouraging and facilitating participation by service-disabled veteran businesses in competitions for the award of agency contracts, and encouraging agency contractors to sub-contract with service-disabled veteran businesses and to actively monitor and evaluate agency contractors' efforts to do so.

But one thing needs to be stressed: This program is available to small businesses that are owned not just by disabled veterans but, very specifically, by service-disabled veterans. The disability must have occurred while serving and in the line of duty. To be considered a service-disabled veteran, the veteran must have an adjudication letter from the Department of Veterans Affairs, a Department of Defense Form 214, Certificate of Release or Discharge from Active Duty, or a Statement of Service from the National Archives and Records Administration stating that the veteran has a service-connected disability.

The purpose of these contracting goals is to help qualifying small businesses become established and develop a track record so that they can compete on an even footing for future contracts. The hope is, for instance, that 8(a) companies will grow out of the program. The experience of Bob Wright and his Dimensions International, Inc. is an example of how the program should work.

"After I finished my stint in the government in the early 1980s, I decided to start a consulting firm doing business development and helping companies get through the maze of doing business with the government," Wright remembers. "But after awhile, I decided to get more into the government sector myself, and I began to look at going after government contracts.

"I started to operate as an 8(a) company and I worked really hard to be a success story. It was important to me that I be a model to show that the program was to give a company a hand up, and to give the company the opportunity to be exposed to the government sector and to learn how to market and to learn how to write proposals. Now, it's 20-plus years later, and I think we've done all right."

Considering the company is doing about $200 million annually and has about 1,500 employees around the world, "all right" would seem to be a bit of an understatement.

Mercedes LaPorta also used the 8(a) program to help get Mercedes Electric Supply Company established.

"When I started 28 years ago, mine was a very, very male-dominated industry," she remembers. "Eventually, the atmosphere started changing, and once I got certified as a minority-owned business, doors started opening up for me because they had to. After I began to develop relationships, and customers began to know me and my company, it became a lot easier. But in the early years, I spent a lot of time just knocking my head against a concrete wall."

Private Sector

Just as the federal government (and most state and local governments) want to do business with small business, so do most of the nation's major corporations. They want to do so for a number of different reasons: Some recognize that small business is a major driver of our economy and anything they do to foster small business helps the economy as a whole, and anything that helps the economy eventually helps them. Others view small business as a major customer of theirs, so helping small business directly helps them. Still others are subject to a bit of arm-twisting because the federal government requires its prime contractors to set goals to give a certain percentage of their subcontracts to small businesses and the government closely monitors the prime contractor's compliance with their subcontracting plans.

FedEx is one of the all-time great small business success stories. It has emerged not only as one of the world's greatest entrepreneurial legends, but as a leader focusing on diversity and on assistance for small businesses. Small business is the customer, the vendor, the ally, and the beneficiary of corporate procurement at FedEx. They have been a leader and a co-sponsor of the SBA's Business Matchmaking events to bring government and corporate contracting opportunities to smaller firms throughout the country. Dennis Taylor is FedEx's point-person in the endeavor. He says:

> As a major contractor for the federal government, we have a number of goals for contracting with small business that are set by the government. But we are finding in the marketplace, more and more, our commercial customers are asking for the same (goals). We have found that having a very aggressive supplier development program is a precursor for doing business.
>
> We have a number of categories where small businesses are supplying software, promotional products—things like logo apparel—and staffing augmentation items. There's one unusual item called "blue juice," the disinfectant that is found in aircraft lavatories. We buy it from a small minority-owned company in Memphis called Memphis Chemical, or as we call them, the "Blue Juice Company."
>
> Any company that comes to us with a quality product, shows us a track record of outstanding service, and is competitive in price is going to get our attention. If it's a large company or a small company, we are going to talk seriously to them. It's a level playing field.

Earlier in this chapter, Dan Sturdivant explained that the federal government and each of its agencies has a procurement process and that any company hoping to do business with that agency needs to learn and understand that process and then follow it. When you talk with the procurement experts from major corporations, they also stress this—that each has a process and if you hope to do business with them, you need to learn, understand, and then follow that process.

FedEx's Dennis Taylor says:

> We have a process in place that some small companies may view as an obstacle, but we and other large companies just follow a program—a procedure—and for 33 years we have been quite successful with that. The best way to learn about this process is to access our web site, www.Fedex.com, click on "About FedEx" and then click on "Contact Us." Under "Vendors & Suppliers," several pages will open, including a discussion about what we buy, how we buy, and what we are looking for. It provides an application to get included in our database. This is the easiest way to get some recognition.

Taylor speaks for most major corporations when you ask him to give a few tips to a small business that might be thinking about selling to FedEx or any large corporation:

> I think the number one thing is to do some homework. You would be surprised at the kinds of things people call FedEx and try to sell us. For instance, a couple of months ago someone called and wanted to sell us shampoo. I assured them we used shampoo, but we don't buy it as a company. Then there was the time a very nice woman called to set up an appointment. She came in and proceeded to try to sell prayer kneelers. Again, I know many of our people use them, but it is one thing I don't buy. So it was a waste of her time and mine.
>
> Second, try to build a relationship. To do that, you need to be persistent. I don't mean persistent to the point you call every day; just use good common business sense. People want to do business with people they have a relationship with.
>
> Finally, you need to have some kind of technology savviness. We have a number of e-tools we use in procurement. So you need to have some kind of overview of technology as it relates to the world of procurement.

Aflac, is another U.S.-global entrepreneurial success story. Today, it is a giant international enterprise, but it started with just three employees. Aflac is another champion of small business widely known for its across-the-board commitment to small business and to supplier diversity. Paul Shelby Amos is Aflac's president and chief operating officer. He says working with small business is an integral part of what Aflac is.

"We have made our mark by helping small businesses. Our rates and the things that we do apply not only to the largest of companies but also to the smallest of companies. We apply them equally across the board. Additionally, because small companies are the fabric of success in America today, and represent the largest volume of employers, we realize that is the largest market opportunity for us. It's really a win–win situation, and we want to be the very best marketer we can be."

"We buy everything from catering to computers," Amos answers when asked what products and services Aflac buys from small businesses. "Almost every service we have falls into one of two categories: technology or facilities. From the nature of our business, we reach out throughout the United States for the procurement business and so we are not limited to the small business base only in our home state of Georgia. We use small businesses throughout the country and we really access them for anything and everything that we need."

He also relates that the company has a special commitment to diversity in its procurement process:

> We see a huge need for diversity whether it's in the workplace or in the procurement process. We not only track directly the number of people we are using from a minority and diversity perspective within our procurement contracts, but we also look at it from two perspectives—the number of people who are doing it directly and the number of people who are doing it indirectly.
>
> I'll give you a couple of examples. We have a contract with Staples whereby we buy a lot of our products from them. One of the things they do for us is to use minority vendors to purchase those products we are outsourcing. Additionally, we are about to build the largest project in the state of Georgia for 2,000 employees in the next five years. In that project, we are requiring all our contractors to have a minimum of 10 percent of their workforce or 10 percent of their subcontracts procured through minority agencies.
>
> We think this is reflective of our employee population that is 70 percent female and 40 percent African American. We absolutely have a huge commitment to both. We believe that by securing 10 percent of our products and services from minority- and female-owned businesses, we are matching that number. We think it is a duty we need to provide to small businesses and especially to those diversity companies out there today.

The advice Amos gives to a small business owner who might be anxious to do business with Aflac is much the same as Dennis Taylor gives to one wanting to do business with FedEx or Dan

Sturdivant gives to the small business owner wanting to do business with the federal government:

> The best way to start doing business with Aflac is to register at our web site *http://aflac.adaptone.com*. All they need to do is go in and put in their NACIS codes and we'll automatically forward their information to the area within our business that handles their particular product.
>
> We suggest they get certified by the SBA or another accredited agency. This gives a tremendous amount of credibility to their business. If they have any type of accreditation, they'll want to be sure they include their references.
>
> It's not necessary for a small business wanting to do business with Aflac to be a certain size or have certain finances, but like any responsible company, we want to make sure a seller can deliver on time and on budget. So when you seek out a contract with Aflac, be prepared to demonstrate your capability and your expertise.
>
> We encourage everyone to go to *http://aflac.adaptone.com* and register today. We use this system and information is forwarded to all our interested parties. The next phase of our web site is to automate the request for proposal process, so all these people can gain access to the system and bid on any of the projects we may have. Ultimately, we want contact them because we are looking for the best possible solution and we may not know what small businesses offer and, if they weren't contacting us, we wouldn't know how to get the best possible vendor.

I have used FedEx and Aflac as examples because of their deep commitment to doing business with small business. But they are just examples of literally hundreds of major corporations that have very active small business procurement programs and that have the same commitment toward those programs that FedEx and Aflac do.

They want to do business with you, but in the end it all comes back to what Dan Sturdivant says: "Four things drive business: process, relationships, homework, and niche versus need." It's that way at federal agencies, and it's that way at Fortune 500 companies.

My former boss, President George W. Bush used to say, "The role of government is not to create wealth or jobs. Small business does that. The role of government is to create an environment where small business is willing to take a risk, an environment to risk their capital, an environment that heralds and celebrates the contributions of America's small business."

He is right.

11

Overcoming the Intimidation Hurdle

THE BUSINESS MATCHMAKING FORMULA

If anyone had come to me in the early days of my small business career and suggested I fly to Washington, DC, to knock on the door of the Department of Defense to try to sell something, I would have laughed and quickly dismissed the idea. The thought of the red tape, the wasted days, the cost of travel, and the unlikelihood that I would even see a decision maker added up to a big dose of intimidation— one that I had no appetite or time for. It would have been humiliating to say the least and, at most, like looking for a needle in a haystack.

During the five years that I traveled the United States asking tens of thousands of small businesses to try something new, to take a bold stance and to open new doors, I found that same sense of intimidation, seasoned with frustration, existed not only in very small start-ups but also among entrepreneurs whose businesses were running well and who were looking for new markets. Right or wrong, fair or not, the climate facing a small business wanting to do business with the government or a Fortune 500 company had not changed all that much between the time I was a young, energetic business owner and when I became SBA administrator with a responsibility to some 25 million small companies throughout our country.

The challenge became a very personal campaign for me. There had to be a way to open the door for deserving companies and make the process affordable, effective, and efficient. And I had some new ammunition. President Bush had taken the lead by insisting that all federal agencies allocate a substantial portion of their purchasing budgets to contracts for small business. Beyond that, there were guidelines in place for special opportunities for minority-, women-, and disabled-veteran-owned small firms.

There is a huge pot of gold. As I mentioned earlier, my last year at the SBA, the federal government's purchasing from small business was $80 billion, up from $50 billion when I started in 2001. I was in a good position to prod each agency along to reach their goals, and I found, in most cases, they were more than willing to reach out, not with a handout, but with a helping hand to small businesses that were qualified. Small business owners are rightly proud. They don't expect anything to be handed to them. They want a hand up not a handout.

Leaders from most federal agencies, like the Department of Homeland Security's Dan Sturdivant, went out of their way to let small companies know they wanted to do business. At the same time, the other good news was that many of the nation's leading corporations were becoming committed to creating opportunities for small business—not by mandate, but because it was the right thing to do and good for business.

Frankly, many opportunities for small businesses start out because they are politically correct, but grow in importance and become standard-bearers because the big companies or government agencies that offered the opportunity find that it is good for their businesses. More often than not, the small firm delivers on time, on budget, and with excellent quality control. Sometimes it's more efficient and cost-effective to do business with a small business.

I learned that from executives at firms like Lockheed, where Gary Bailey and Sam Evans and their team make sure that the giant prime contractor has a team of small entrepreneurs involved in every project. I heard the same from Brian Tippens at Hewlett-Packard (HP), Dennis Taylor at FedEx, and Bill Mullahy and Mike Robinson at Aflac. Their message was consistent. Buying from small business has become a solid benefit for the buyer and not just the seller.

Now the challenge was getting this message out around the country. The mood was changing: The federal agency mandate was in place. Major corporations were coming on board. But there was still the time and distance problem. How could any small business owner in Denver, Phoenix, Atlanta, or Kansas City afford to take the time, and to spend the money, to fly to Washington, DC, or to some Fortune 500 corporate office with the hope of justifying that time and financial commitment by making a sale? As my dad put it, "Small business has the know-how, they just need to know who."

When I was leading the Latin Business Association (LBA), we created an event called the LBA Expo. Our members said they wanted contracts from the large corporations, and unless we were able to provide them those opportunities, they would not continue being members of the organization. Because of those demands, we created a business matchmaking initiative.

In the beginning, the large corporations and small businesses weren't sure it would work. We devoted a considerable amount of time, energy, and resources to make sure that we got results. It turned out to be a huge success. When I went to Washington and heard all of the complaints of small business about how difficult it was to do business with the government, we took the concept that we created at the business association and built on it to create what is now the Business Matchmaking program. Small business wants the same thing that big business wants—more business. If you can find a way for small business to access these contracts, they will beat a path to your door.

The LBA program was only a pilot program, but it worked and it proved to me the concept was right and was scalable. Now I had the opportunity to do it right. I had the resources and the relationships to make access affordable and quick for small business owners anywhere in the country. That's how Business Matchmaking was born.

The idea was simple. Create a road show and visit different parts of the country. Get all those Dan Sturdivants and Dennis Taylors, purchasing executives from government and from industry, to travel to the hometowns of the small business owners, and go face-to-face with them and have contracts on the table. You can't and shouldn't guarantee anyone a contract, but you can give them access and a level playing field and that's a lot.

We started with a few pilot sessions to get the kinks out. One problem was the lack of preparation by the entrepreneurs. Too many small business owners were showing up grateful for the opportunity to meet a real buyer from a federal agency, but unable to succinctly and effectively talk about their products or services and make the case for a sale. It quickly became apparent that training was needed, and counselors would have to get involved. I needed a partner in the private sector—preferably a company that was not only committed to the Business Matchmaking concept, but one that was able to deliver the resources to launch and grow the concept.

I met two individuals who were to become central to the Business Matchmaking concept and to me personally. Chuck Ashman, a marketing expert and media producer with a client base of companies that wanted to penetrate the small business arena, and Diane Kegley, a former C-Net executive who had been in the forefront of the dot-com revolution.

We talked and it became immediately apparent that we had something very much in common. Here were two private sector leaders passionate about bringing big companies to the small business table, while I was immersed in doing the same with government agencies. Literally, in a matter of days, meetings were taking place between my staff and senior officials at HP, the computer giant.

Hewlett-Packard became an original founder of Business Matchmaking and was probably the most important private sector participant in terms of launching the initiative. I often said that HP not only provided the financial resources to create and underwrite all of the Business Matchmaking events but also the technology for the small businesses attending. They always brought their procurement representatives with contracts in hand to be offered to the small businesses in attendance who were the right fit for HP's needs.

No other company did as much in the beginning. Hewlett-Packard said they wanted to be known in the small business community as the small business technology go-to company. They took a long-term view and worked diligently to change the perception that HP was only for large corporations. Five years later, I believe they are well on their way to achieving their goals in the small business community.

And, talk about a good fit. HP had started in a garage in northern California and their current leadership never forgot that humble beginning. Compaq, their huge Texas acquisition, had actually opened its doors thanks to financing facilitated by the SBA.

In the months that followed, we shared ideas and resources and came up with a plan: Part one was taking the show on the road. We would go to Pasadena and Anaheim, California. We would visit Orlando, Florida, and Atlanta, Georgia. We would schedule major events in Houston, Texas; Milwaukee, Wisconsin; Chicago, Illinois; Denver, Colorado; and in other key cities in every region of the country.

It was important that no small business be charged anything for the experience. The SBA and their private sector partner HP would present it all without fee for the entrepreneur.

Now that still left the intimidation problem. Too many really fine small firms did not realize they could open the door for their own growth by selling to important customers coming to them from federal agencies and corporate offices around the nation. So I enlisted help from SCORE.

Ken Yancey, its CEO, understood the concept instantly and jumped in. SCORE became an indispensable partner by providing counselors at the Business Matchmaking events to help those small firms maneuver into the world of government contracts, remaining available to mentor as new relationships were created.

Things worked so well that when the period of SBA sponsorship was completed, SCORE and HP were able to continue and grow the program, bringing onboard outstanding private sector partners like American Airlines, Aflac, FedEx, AT&T, Research In Motion (RIM), MasterCard, and other leaders in their respective industries.

Small Business Administration speakers and panelists are still very active in the Business Matchmaking events, joining the SCORE and HP team in making the time spent at Matchmaking by any entrepreneur more than worthwhile.

I traveled to the regional Business Matchmaking events and met with the media that focus on issues affecting small business. My message was always the same. It was no longer necessary to be intimidated. The red tape was fading. The training and counseling was available. The buyers were coming to the sellers. We were off and running with no plans to look back.

We needed one more essential element—a 24/7 connector to keep things hot between Business Matchmaking regional events. The Internet was the obvious environment, but we needed a very customized web solution.

Enter Bob Wright's Dimensions International, Inc. (DI), which developed the program that would enable the right seller to go face-to-face with the right buyer. Before this remarkable solution, a buyer and a seller both interested in apparel might be scheduled to meet. The problem was the buyer needed hats and the seller only sold socks. DI's Business Matchmaking technology (*www.businessmatchmaking.com*) ensured that only the right buyers and sellers were matched. This proprietary technology has raised the bar and has become the industry standard for these kinds of buyer-seller relationships.

SMA Global, Chuck Ashman's and Diane Kegley's company, produces Business Matchmaking, using DI's technology to provide constant access to training and essential intelligence for small companies in the program. In some cases, actual buyer-seller sessions are set up via the Web even without the regular regional events.

Often small businesses say, "Even if I could get the appointments, which I probably couldn't; it would take me a year to do what I can do in a day or two at Matchmaking." If you canvassed the more than 50,000 small companies that have had face-to-face selling sessions in the Business Matchmaking program, I know you would find a great many who had to overcome the intimidation factor to get there. While being in the door is no guarantee of a sale, it always is the essential first step.

With $750 million in contracts awarded so far, those small businesses know firsthand what I hope all of you reading this will come to accept: There are commonsense ways to prepare for opportunities. There are times when being bold and taking a chance can deliver incredible results. Finally, take care of the basics. For example, here a few of the established lessons of the Business Matchmaking initiative:

1. *Be able to describe your company simply, precisely, and quickly.* Many call that the *elevator pitch* version. It should only take a minute to let someone know what you do.

2. *Be ready to reference some of those customers you have served.* Also, be ready to back up the reference with contact information. Even if the buyer doesn't make the call, offering the information adds to your credibility.

3. *Never be on time; always be a little early.* Get the lay of the land and become familiar with exactly where you are going, who you are meeting with, and what the situation is like.

4. *Research, research, and then research.* Before you take a meeting with a buyer from any government agency or major corporation, do your homework. Look at their web site, read their press releases, and focus on their supplier programs and practices. A face-to-face 15-minute meeting is no place to ask a company or government agency what they need. You should know that going in the door.

5. *Follow up is critical.* Yes, there is a balance between effective follow-up and being a "pain in the neck!" Ask at the end of any meeting, ask, "When may I call you?" or "Do you prefer e-mail or a phone call to follow up?"

6. *Network whenever you can.* We have found that individual small firms cannot handle a particular opportunity, but by combining with other small firms, they can do the job. These regional events and the Matchmaking Online Network are great ways to meet others who may complement your company and work with you to secure a contract.

The most important thing about the Matchmaking concept is that it works. It works for the small businesses seeking contracts, and it works for the corporations and government agencies that are looking for qualified small businesses with which to do business.

Country Bake of Fairburn, Georgia, is an eight-person commercial bakery that specializes in frozen dough biscuits and fully baked biscuits in various flavors. It sells to large food wholesalers and first-tier distributors whose clients are restaurants, institutional customers like schools, business cafeterias, the military, and food stores.

Danny Gardner is Country Bake's owner. He has become a big fan of Business Matchmaking after the success he encountered in March 2005 in Nashville.

"I had heard about the Matchmaking process and when I heard it was going to be in Nashville, I signed up. But I didn't really know what to expect, being our first experience with Matchmaking. We had been told about the one-on-one, face-to-face, opportunities, but we thought it was going to be similar to other conferences we had been to."

But when he got to Nashville, he realized that he had the opportunity to meet directly, and alone, with buyers. He remembers, "When I saw commercial food distributor Robert Orr Sysco Corp. on the list of buyers, I got excited because we had been trying to get in front of major wholesalers like them, and I saw it as a tremendous opportunity."

Gardner traveled to Nashville with product literature and targeted this one buyer. After just a few minutes of conversation with their purchasing agent, Gardner felt he had made a connection and that he had a chance to turn this interview into a real selling opportunity. He says, "The relationship began to blossom immediately. They saw we had a product that could fit into their menu lineup, and we were able to proceed from there."

As with most Matchmaking situations, the one-on-one gave Gardner and Country Bake not an instant contract, but rather a foot in a new door and for them a very valuable new door. Gardner followed up the initial meeting with several phone conversations with the buyer, and this led shortly to a second trip to Nashville when Gardner brought product samples.

"Essentially, they set up a test to compare our product to their leading brand and they found they liked our product better. Then we made a second trip back and they took us out to meet one of their biggest customers and to show our product to them. The customer liked what they tasted, and we were in business."

That initial Matchmaking meeting has led to an $80,000 contract, and more important, an introduction into the Sysco system nationally. The end result was not only a recurring contract with the company but also additional contacts with its customers. Gardner believes that has potential for a large amount of new business down the road.

But he cautions that the initial face-to-face Matchmaking meeting is really only the start of a process that can lead to new business for a seller.

"The one-on-one is an opportunity to see if there is synergy, an opportunity to see if there was a match between what we offer and what Sysco Corp. was looking for. We identified very quickly in that one-on-one that there was a match. The next step then was the follow-up. The follow-up has to take place, and you have to be aggressive. The Matchmaking gave us the platform to identify where an opportunity might exist. But you have to have product, you have to have pricing, and you have to have the ability to close the deal."

If there is a Business Matchmaking superstar, it is unquestionably Best Products Company of Houston, Texas. Run by Donnie McDaniel and his wife Claire, Best Products was at the very first Matchmaking event and has been to every one since—except one—and they can point to $14 million in contracts they have gotten based on contacts first made at Matchmaking.

Best Products is not a giant enterprise. It started in April 1998 as a distributor of janitorial supplies and office supplies (today, Best Products distributes a wide range of office, janitorial, and industrial supplies). By 2000, they were doing what, at the time, was a phenomenal $100,000 a year in business.

A fortunate happenstance for Donnie McDaniel was that the first Business Matchmaking event took place in his hometown of Houston, also one of the two homes of HP. It essentially was love at first sight, both for McDaniel and for many of the purchasing executives he met with.

McDaniel has come back to Matchmaking event after Matchmaking event, no matter where in the country it has been held, and at every event he comes away with new contacts that he has turned into new contracts.

"We started our business with $15,000 in the bank with one employee," Donnie McDaniel says. "Our total sales in 2000 were $100,000. Now we have 26 employees, and did $14 million last year."

McDaniel keeps a list of the companies he now does business with, or has done business with, based on a first contact made at Matchmaking. There are 117 in all, ranging from federal to state to local governmental agencies, public sector enterprises like hospitals, and many, many of America's top corporations. He says, "Having the opportunity to get in front of major prime buyers and talk about your products and service is 90 percent of the battle. It does not mean you will get a contract. It only positions you to compete for a contract."

We always tell the small businesses that come to Matchmaking that what they are involved in is the start of a process. We tell them they have 15 minutes to spend with a purchasing officer and that after that short time do not expect to walk away with a sale or with a contract. What you should do is present your company, its products or services, and your credentials; see if what you are offering is a good fit for what they are buying; and learn a bit about their purchasing process—as we have seen elsewhere in these pages, all big companies, just like the government, have a very specific process that has to be followed. Then you must follow up, follow up, follow up, and hopefully what you start at Matchmaking will result in a sale or contract down the road.

That is what happened to Country Bake, and Donnie McDaniel has learned this lesson well. Dan Sturdivant says when dealing with a federal agency or buying arm, prepare to wait six months. We say over and over don't expect to walk away from that table with a contract—and then at a Matchmaking event in Orlando, Florida, I saw it happen.

Florida, with its hurricanes, presents unique problems for institutions like hospitals. One of the biggest, I have come to learn, is potable water. A hurricane hits, the hospital loses power then goes to backup power, but it also may have its incoming water supply either cut off or contaminated. It is a big problem, a very big problem.

I was told by a hospital purchasing manager who was at the Matchmaking session meeting with small businesses that what the hospital would do when a hurricane was forecast was fill buckets with water—a lot of buckets. "But, they quickly get contaminated," he told me, so the hospital was looking for some better way.

Along came a woman entrepreneur, who with her husband had invented and were selling a plastic device that held five gallons of clean drinking water, which actually could be worn around a person's neck, with the water dispensed as needed through several kinds of tubes.

Talk about a match made in heaven, or maybe more correctly somebody having a niche that almost exactly fit a buyer's need. The first question the buyer asked was a simple: "How many can you deliver to me, and when?"

So maybe it doesn't happen often. But I guess we learned, at least as far as Business Matchmaking is concerned, to never say never.

Matchmaking works well for the companies who come to take advantage of meeting face-to-face with qualified small businesses with which there is a mutual interest.

American Airlines reaches out to small business around the country and the world. Entrepreneurs are their customers, suppliers, and partners. They were among the first major corporations to join HP in the early stages of the Business Matchmaking initiative.

As this book is going to press, American Airlines has just awarded another major contract to a very small business owner they met face-to-face at the Southeastern Business Matchmaking event in Atlanta, Georgia, earlier this year.

Roger Frizzell, their vice president, oversees American's sponsorship of the Business Matchmaking and diversity-related events. He summed it up by saying, "Business Matchmaking has provided us with a remarkable opportunity to meet with small business owners throughout the country. The program is efficient, economical, easy, and very effective. We continue to expand our role because of the positive results we see as a sponsor."

We have already met FedEx's Dennis Taylor, one of the deans of the private sector procurement team that meets face-to-face with small business owners all over the country. He has been a pioneer in the development of the Business Matchmaking initiative and knows firsthand why it works.

"The key to these events is the quality and quantity of the small business owners a corporation meets," Taylor says. "At our most recent event in Atlanta, Georgia, more than 200 small business Matchmaking participants signed up for our new program and there are more in the pipeline. That is a really remarkable achievement. These Matchmaking events help us meet and create relationships with customers, potential vendors, and even alliance partners. It works well across the board."

So now you know. We built it, now it's up to you.

Good luck and good selling!

12

Demystifying Capital and Getting Financial Help

California politician Jesse Unruh once said, "Money is the mother's milk of politics." It's the same for small business. It's the air they breathe.

Former Congressman Jack Kemp likes to say that capital is like oxygen: it's what small businesses need to breathe, grow their business, start their business, or take their business to the next level. I believe that's true. They need money to start, grow, and build long-term success.

Access to capital has always been one of the biggest issues and challenges confronting small business. When my parents started their businesses, they were always undercapitalized and had to put bandages on many pressing problems because of a lack of capital. Often, small businesses are scrambling or robbing Peter to pay Paul. I faced this in my own business, and I heard countless complaints from members of the business organizations I was a member of and from those I led.

Linn Wiley has long been one of California's outstanding bankers. He is the former president and chief executive officer of CVB Financial Corp. and Citizens Business Bank since 1991. The Bank is one of the largest in Southern California with 30 offices and approximately $2.3 billion in assets.

Before heading Citizens Business Bank, Wiley, a U.S. Marine Corps veteran, was executive vice president of Wells Fargo Bank, president of American National Bank, and executive vice president of Lloyds Bank California (now Sanwa Bank of California). At one time, he was California's youngest bank president; he has sat on the board of directors of the Los Angeles Branch of the Federal Reserve Bank of San Francisco. Now, he is taking on the challenge of starting a new bank in Las Vegas.

His many years in banking have given him both expertise and insights into the capitalization problems not only of start-up new small businesses, but also of fast-growing and expanding enterprises. He says:

> The mistakes I see are often of a financial nature. People have a product or an idea that they are really enamored with. They can be very good at developing a product. They might be very good even at marketing that product. But they just don't give the proper attention to the financial side of the business.
>
> To start with, most businesses start out undercapitalized. I tell people to figure out how much capital they need and then multiply by three because that's how much is usually necessary. Then, everybody wants to grow. But you have to have the working capital to grow. If your inventory and receivables grow faster than your cash flow, then you can't pay your bills.
>
> A business needs to be objective about its growth plans. The number one reason I believe that new businesses fail is they start without enough capital. You have to have money to make money. Some people will start and become very successful, but then they outgrow their resources. There is a phrase that's used: "You can't grow broke." If your receivables are growing faster than your sales, then you don't have the cash flow to support the growth. You have to collect those receivables. It's the cash that allows you to grow the receivables. Another factor is if you're growing your receivables that quickly, you don't have the money to replenish your inventory, if you're the kind of business that depends on inventory.
>
> This is something that people don't give sufficient weight to, whether they're just entering business or when they're relatively new in business.

In writing this book, I talked with a great many successful entrepreneurs, most of whom started out as small business owners. Most shared a common experience—lack of capital when they started out and often lack of capital at critical stages of growth of their companies when they were poised to move to the next level. Mercedes LaPorta said, in describing the growth of her electrical supply business:

> In the years I've been in business, there's been many difficult moments we've had to overcome—financial problems, times when we would have growth spurts and didn't have the proper financing in place. When you are getting ready to make that next leap, to significantly grow your business up to the next level, you simply must have the proper financial backing. You need to have your financing in place, because your initial outlay of funds to gather the resources you're going to need, whatever they may be for your business, is going to cost you money. Most likely, you're not going to see a return on that investment for a considerable time. It could be years before you see any return come back. So you have to have that kind of backing to get you through that period. And it takes planning for you to avoid big problems and headaches. In some cases, people have tried to do this and have not been able to overcome this problem, have not had the financing in place, and have seen their businesses fail.

At TELACU, David Lizarraga deals with small business owners every day, and every day he sees the same problems:

> One of the principal problems that a new small business owner has is under capitalization. Many businesses start and hope they're going to get the money they need as the business develops. Instead, they run out of money and they're never able to realize the full potential of the business. It can take two or three years to get a business up and running and profitable and many people starting businesses are not ready for this amount of time before their businesses become sufficiently established.

Securities broker-dealer Harold Doley couldn't agree more:

> I think the biggest challenge for somebody starting out in business is the fact that nothing happens as fast as you might like. So the biggest risk you have is being undercapitalized. And the idea of praying that you're going to make it quicker isn't going to help you. That's going to lead to putting you in great financial risk.
>
> The other problem is overestimating your own capabilities. Sometimes people read these success stories that are at least in part fictionalized,

in my opinion. So they think they can do it and max out their credit cards and they wind up broke. Or they pursue a deal in blind faith that doesn't make any sense. They may have a product that they believe in, but nobody wants it. As a friend of mine once said, "Nobody goes broke doing a bad deal they go broke chasing a bad deal."

So you are a new small business owner and you know you need start-up capital. Where do you go? Linn Wiley, based on his years in banking, has a suggestion and a warning:

You need to come in with a good, thorough business plan. What appeals to a lot of people in starting a business is the product or service and their own sales or marketing abilities and they ignore the financial aspects of the business. What I tell people, and I don't think a lot of people understand, is that in our business we have a unique responsibility to make only those loans that are viable and to not make loans that are not viable. It's important to make the loans that we think can be supported because that not only helps the person or business but it helps the general economy. Conversely, if we make loans that are not viable, it hurts both the individual and the economy. You wouldn't have to go through the whole distasteful collection process and the litigation if the bank never made the loan in the first place.

For many years, Rudolph I. "Rudy" Estrada was the district director of the Small Business Administration's (SBA) Los Angeles district, the largest SBA district in the nation.

He is now president and chief executive officer of Estradagy, a business and financial services company providing comprehensive advisory assistance to the business, banking, and public services sectors. Estradagy has been retained by more than 60 commercial banks to help them, among other things, set up small business loan programs. Rudy also teaches banking and finance and is one of the most knowledgeable people I know in the area of small business finance. He says:

I used to firmly believe there was a lack of capital out there, a lack of access to capital for small businesses starting up. Typically, you hear the banks will only loan money to people who don't need it. But in the past 10 years, banks have begun to focus on the opportunities that are available in financing start-up businesses. It has become such a feeding frenzy in providing capital for firms in the middle of the upper reaches that banks have begun to develop a less risk adverse attitude, and they are now willing to dig deeper to make financing available to companies that they weren't financing earlier.

But Rudy Estrada echoes the same kind of warning as Linn Wiley:

> If you have a promising business, you will get financing. If you exhibit the kind of potential a banker wants to see, you will get a loan. But if you don't, no one is in the business of providing you with free money. That's called granting, and it really doesn't exist.
>
> You're always going to have this dilemma of lack of capital for small companies who cannot evidence a future. You can't expect a doctor to die with his patients, yet we often expect banks to bend over backward to fund businesses that show no promise. I think it's unfair to put banks in that position.

Bob d'Augustino, one of the New York area's most experienced SCORE counselors, specializes in getting a new small business owner ready to ask for financing, and then actually taking him and introducing him to a lender who might be predisposed to making a loan. He says:

> After a perspective new small business owner has completed our classes, received the written certificate we give him, and written a business plan, he is ready to go in front of a lender.
>
> We teach and counsel the importance of preparing a cash flow projection and tell him how important the three Cs are. I tell him that when you're starting a new business, you have to show the banker that you have your three Cs: C for collateral, C for cash flow, and C for credit.
>
> You have to show that, starting with month number one when you get your loan, the very first month even if your business has no income, you can pay them. So where is the money coming from? And since you're a new small business, they can only judge you by your existing credit. They cannot judge you by your track record—you have none. So those three Cs are critical for the start-up business.
>
> If you have an existing business, it's easier because I could tell them we still need your credit report and we still need some collateral, but instead of cash flow we can show them your tax returns for the past year or two so the bank can get some idea of where you stand financially—what your financial record is. Instead of a projection, you have a record now, and that will help the bank make a decision.
>
> In the past 33 months, I've gotten over $14 million for our clients, just in our one chapter.

Bob d'Augustino makes a critically important point when he talks about banks. All banks are different, different in how they do business, and—the key point—different in who they like to lend money to. You could have a start-up business with the best business plan in the world, and if you go into a bank that only lends to businesses that have been in business for two years, you're out of luck. Likewise, no matter what your experience if you are opening a new restaurant and you go into a bank that considers start-up restaurants to be too big of a risk, again you're out of luck. In either case, you don't get the loan through no fault of your own.

D'Augustino says that he picks and chooses carefully which banks the owner or potential owner should go to:

> We first ask where they now bank, where are they known by a bank. And they'll usually tell us, "Well, we have a family checking account and a savings account." I ask them the name of the bank and I evaluate it. I know most of the banks in the New York metropolitan area, and I'll tell them, "Well, this bank is not really a good bank for a small business loan." I don't want to paint a rosy picture that's false. Or I'll say, "Oh, this bank is on my list as being a good bank to approach."
>
> We break up the banks in the New York area specifically by what areas of lending they seem to enjoy. For example, we have a bank, Country Bank, in New York that likes to make loans to restaurants. Now restaurants have notoriously high failure records. Restaurants are known as the highest risk small business, but here we have a bank that likes to take a chance with restaurants because their loan officer is an experienced restaurateur.
>
> I try to match the client with the bank. Right away, I've increased the chance of minimizing the risk for this loan. Second, if I look at their three Cs and find that they're very weak with their credit, or they have no collateral, and they have no way of meeting the payments on their loan because they're a start-up and it will take them several months to have some cash flow, they can't meet any of the three Cs, then I've developed an alternative list of community-based lenders.
>
> In the New York area, we have about 15 community-based lenders that are not banks. They've gotten their money from banks, or it has been donated to them by various organizations. For example, if I have a Hispanic coming in to see me who needs some start-up money, but he doesn't have the three Cs that are required by an institutional lender like a bank, I'll take him to a community-based lender called "Accion" (Action) in the Bronx, New York. They like to loan money to Hispanic

small business start-ups or owners because they've historically been dis-
criminated against. They've obtained money from various sources, mostly
donations, and they give or loan that money to Latinos who want to start
a small business.

Or if I'm interested in helping a woman who cannot get money
from a bank because she doesn't have the three Cs, I'll go to the Women's
Enterprise Fund in Tarrytown, New York. They specialize in helping
women who want to start a small business and don't require the three Cs.
They give what is essentially a character loan, instead of a minimum risk
loan, as a bank wants. A character loan is just basically taking a chance on
an individual based on a hopeful business plan, an interview that shows
that this person really wants to try very hard but just doesn't have the
requisites to qualify for a bank loan. They'll go as high as $25,000 on a
community-based lending loan.

There is yet another kind of lender we have not discussed—
the venture capitalist. As Bob d'Augustino notes, this is a very
different kind of lender:

If I've got a client that comes in who I think has a chance of getting venture capital, I've got a unique situation. The venture capitalists are really
pretty tough guys to deal with. If they think you have a great idea, they pretty
much want (most of them anyway) to eventually take over the business
from you. But in the meantime, they are willing to put their money at
risk. They have money that they are willing to lose, but they'll be looking
over your shoulder pretty carefully.

I've gone through a number of venture capital sources, and I've come
up with two that I use frequently because they're so predictable, honest,
and responsive to the SCORE clients we send to them. The first is the
National Venture Capital Association in Arlington, Virginia; their web site
is NVCA.org. They are an organization that specializes in locating, iden-
tifying, and investing money in young companies that have an idea, a
service, or a product that they think could go.

The second one is the National Association of Small Business Investment Companies in Washington, DC; their web site is _www.nasbic.org._

However, I warn the client that if they do go with either of these two
organizations, they have to be very careful because the firms will not consider giving them any investment money, unless they think their product
or service is so unique that it has a potential, a real potential, of achieving
multimillion-dollar sales within one to two years.

They're not looking for something that's going to take several years
to develop real sales. They're looking for something that is so good, so
unique, so promising that they're going to see multimillion-dollar income

within a relatively short period of time. If I don't think a client's company meets those criteria, I will tell them you're wasting your time talking to a venture capitalist. If it meets those criteria, I will recommend they contact those two organizations.

Then there are riskier and more expensive ways to get a limited amount of early financing. Bob d'Augustino explains:

As a last resort, if I've really done everything I could and they don't qualify for a bank loan or a community-based loan; they can't get any money from their relatives, friends, or business acquaintances because they just don't have the money to give them; and they've pretty much petered out all their other possibilities, there are a few last resorts.

I will tell them, look, there are companies that have become extremely successful—John Johnson, who started *Ebony* magazine and became a multimillionaire, couldn't get a loan from a bank. He was an African American man who couldn't get a loan from anybody. He sold his mom's furniture for $500 and started *Ebony* magazine with that $500, and now he's a multimillionaire.

If you still want to start that business, and you don't want to wait, then you resort to guerilla tactics for getting money. It means you might have to pay 15 percent, 16 percent, or 19 percent for money on a credit card. If you are sure that the idea is going to fly, but no one else is sure, then resort to high interest borrowing and that means credit cards. It means other forms of borrowing that I don't normally recommend, except as a last resort. But it has been done. It's highly risky, but if they don't want to wait until they're ready, and to prepare themselves with a little more time and a little more training, maybe saving some money, I say well there's always that last-ditch attempt.

When I became the SBA administrator, I resolved to do everything possible to help solve the problem that small businesses have in gaining access to the capital they need so badly. The first thing I did was determine the real numbers regarding loans made and dollars guaranteed. I have always believed that the numbers don't lie. I also wanted to understand what the average loan size was, and who these loans were going to. For example, I questioned how were we doing in the emerging markets or women and minority business communities, the two fastest-growing segments of small business in the United States today.

I found the trends were flat. We were doing fewer than 50,000 loans a year, and had been for some time. The average loan size we were guaranteeing was almost $250,000. That was way too high. If $250,000 was the average, then many were much larger. If the start-up small business goes in and asks for $25,000 or $50,000, they will get turned down because the profit to the bank in a loan that small is just not enough when they have many larger guaranteed loans they could be making.

The numbers in the underserved markets was below average and not commensurate with their market share. I knew we had a lot of work to do, and a major sales job in front of us.

We did something that hadn't been done for some time, if ever. Instead of going to each of our major banking partners separately—we had over 6,000 banks licensed to do SBA loans—we asked them to come to us. We hosted an all-day work session at SBA headquarters with key banking leaders from all across the country representing all types of banking institutions, along with all of our key managers, to discuss how we could increase our business together and accomplish some very aggressive goals.

I started out our presentation by letting these banking executives know of our commitment to doing more small business loans of all types, with a particular emphasis on smaller loans and penetrating the ever-important fast-growing markets. I thought we made a compelling case, but I was surprised what I heard when we asked for their feedback.

The executives were polite, but direct. They told us that they were in business to make a profit and they were not philanthropic organizations. They understood our goals, but could not commit to them because they said it was too bureaucratic and time consuming to do business with the federal government. I asked them for recommendations on how we could cut through the red tape and streamline our process. They gave me a long list of suggestions.

I was frank with them as well. I explained that I came from the private sector and understood that our partnership had to be mutually beneficial. I also told them that we couldn't accomplish everything on their list, but we would focus like a laser beam on their top priorities. What we ended up with was an expansion of a loan program that was specifically targeted to smaller businesses.

The name of that program was SBA Express. In it, we increased the maximum loan to $250,000 from $150,000. This seems a contradiction. But by allowing them to make larger loans on which they made a greater profit, they were more willing to make smaller loans. We also allowed the banks to use their own forms, and if they were a "preferred bank" to make the initial loan approval without SBA approval in advance. They could also transmit required information electronically and, ultimately, we also centralized the loan liquidation process for any loans that were in default. This was important because we had 70 different district offices that had dissimilar processes. This is a killer for a bank that does loans in more than one state.

The changes we made were nothing short of revolutionary and went a long way to saving the banks time and money. "Time is money," and these leaders reminded me that if we could do things quicker and more efficiently, they could be profitable and make many more loans.

At the time, SBA Express was considered a pilot program and represented a small amount of the loans being guaranteed by the SBA. Last year, SBA Express loans represented 60 percent of the SBA loan portfolio. We went on to break loan records every year. The total number of loans went from 50,000 to over 100,000. Dollars guaranteed went from less than $10 billion a year to over $20 billion a year. Loans to women increased by double digits every year and loans to minorities became a third of the portfolio. The average loan size went down from almost $250,000 to about $160,000. These were dramatic results for a government agency that had been stalled in their loan production for years. We've proved that making smaller loans to more small businesses was not only the right thing to do, but a very profitable business for our banking partners. By the way, we still made more large loans than ever before as well. In fact, our portfolio for larger fixed assets and real estate increased from $2.5 billion to over $5 billion during the same time.

The *Wall Street Journal* (April 12, 2007, p. 12) recently carried a fascinating article by staff writer David Enrich. Entitled "Banks Court

Small Businesses," the article on one level gives me great satisfaction because it shows the progress we made in my five years at the SBA in getting big banks to make small business loans. But the article highlights the confusion that still remains in the banking industry over the issue of small business lending. Some banks say it is great and they embrace it. Others question its profitability and avoid, or even, shun it.

Reading this well-crafted article, the problem is clear. Some lenders are welcoming small business borrowers with open arms. Others are saying the risk is too great. Some are willing to loan to you if you have been in business for only a day, others want two successful years at a minimum. This only goes to support what Bob d'Augustino found in the New York area: You need to carefully choose which lender you approach.

Because small businesses owners have to sift and choose among banks to find the one most likely to even consider lending to them, I and several like-minded leaders are in the process of establishing a new bank in the dynamic Las Vegas, Nevada, market where the small- and medium-size business segment has been traditionally underserved.

Small business owners need and deserve the same level of banking attention that the richest individuals and the largest corporations are accustomed to. That is the culture we will create in Nevada with our "proposed Prime Bank." First, we will bring our banking to our customers. If they are busy, we will come to them with our services. A loan application, a deposit, and a check being cashed can be done in their office as well as at our bank.

The growth of the Hispanic community in our country has been spectacular and now Nevada leads the way. While we are launching a major initiative to assist Hispanic small business in Nevada, we will also offer the same level of customer service to all constituencies—especially women-owned small businesses, African American and Asian American companies, veteran- and disabled-veteran-owned companies. All communities will receive the same customized service.

My dad used to say that when he went to a bank for a loan they wanted, demanded, and expected a track record, but he said he would never have a track record because they would never give him the track to run on. That's what we were able to accomplish during my tenure at the SBA. We gave some good, deserving small businesses a track.

Interestingly, small businesses that get loans through the SBA come back for a second and third loan. As I said earlier, business is evolutionary. They may start out with a very small loan, but after they pay it back, they may need a much larger loan to satisfy their growing business needs. Later, they may buy expensive equipment or purchase the building they occupy.

For some who grow very large, they may some day be candidates for venture capital, which SBA pioneered for the small business market. Some household names like Staples, Federal Express, America On Line (AOL), and others were recipients of this type of venture capital facilitated by the SBA's investment division.

When I spoke before groups or testified before Congress, I would often be asked what the default rate is on SBA-guaranteed small business loans. The questioners were often surprised when I told them that the experience and exposure is not much different from that of large commercial banks that approve loans without the SBA guarantees. In other words, small businesses have historically performed well in the SBA portfolio. I believe that the work that is done before they come to SBA in terms of business planning and the technical assistance they receive makes a big difference and increases their prospects for success.

I am proud of many things we were able to accomplish, but this revamping and expanding of the loan guarantee had a special satisfaction. I'm happy we helped many entrepreneurs breathe easier.

Maybe we had a small role in starting something that was long overdue. When I started at the SBA, I received some good advice: I was told that the agency was almost 50 years old, and many of the issues I would confront were endemic and I would not be able to resolve them in my time there. They said just endeavor to leave the agency better than when I found it and, if I did that, I would have accomplished something worthwhile.

I have no doubt that in the areas of capital access, entrepreneurial development, and contracting, we accomplished that simple but important objective. I will always be proud that we did.

IV | Summing Up

13

ABCs of Success

In the last chapter, we met California banker D. Linn Wiley. Linn has run businesses—banks—but more importantly he has dealt with small business owners constantly over a 30-year career. The banks he has run have specialized in business lending and especially small business lending. Over the years Linn has developed a special feel for small business and has seen over and over what contributes to a small business' success, and what is often absent in a small business that fails.

He calls these his *ABCs of Small Business Success:*

A is for ATTITUDE.
B is for BELIEVE.
C is for COMMITMENT.
D is for DEDICATION.
E is for EXECUTION and for ENTHUSIASM.
F is for FOCUS.

"I have what I call the ABCs of business," Linn told me. "The most important component of being successful is having a great *attitude*. It's always looking for way to be successful and not getting bogged down in adversity.

"Everything begins with attitude. If you've got it, you get good results. If you have a bad attitude, you get bad results. If you have a great attitude, you'll likely get great results; but if your attitude is only so-so, then you'll get just so-so results. I believe that when people wake up in the morning they have several choices. They can make it a great day, or they can make it something less, which rides on how we approach the day.

"You have to feel good about yourself before you can feel good about anything else. First you have to believe in your industry, and the fact that your industry provides real value. Then you have to believe in your company and that your company is an active and contributing part of the industry and that, as a company, you provide value that's not available someplace else.

"Looking at any event, there are things that can go right, and things that can go wrong. So what happens in the event is predicated on how you're approaching it from the inception. I do a lot of sales training, and you might tell people if you're on your way to a sales call you might be thinking that the sales call is going to go right and what you can do to make it go right. Or you might be thinking about the resistance you're going to encounter and why it's going to go wrong. Often, which of those two thought processes you're working under will determine the outcome of a sales call.

"Next most important is you have to *believe* in yourself. You have to believe in yourself because if you don't believe in yourself, then you really can't accomplish anything that's worthwhile. You have to have the confidence in yourself to be able to take chances to be able to make decision that can be wrong. You have to have belief in yourself, belief in what you do, belief in your ability; you have to have this before you can really be successful.

"Then you have to have *commitment*. You have to commit yourself to whatever you are going to do. You can't get distracted and allow yourself to start thinking about other things. You have to be totally focused on what you are doing and you have to have the dedication that allows you to see it through to the fruition. Commitment is when you have a passion for whatever it is you are going to do. You make the commitment; you take the initiative.

"*Dedication* is making sure you follow through. I don't know how many times I've heard people say 'I'm going to do this' and then they don't follow through. Or, you hear people say 'I'm going to do this' and then they add an 'if' and then they throw in every excuse known to man. They set themselves up for failure. For many people half their lives are 'if.' They make contingent commitments. But when you go to establish a business you have to make an absolute commitment and then you have to have the dedication to follow through. A lot of people will get something started but they don't finish it because they don't have the dedication.

"Finally, there's *execution*. No matter how good the plan is, you have to execute for anything good to happen. At the end of the day it's all about execution. Another E is *enthusiasm*. The more enthusiastic you are about something the more influential you're going to be in getting it done.

"All five are connected. Your attitude is going to determine whether you believe in yourself. If you believe in yourself, then you have the confidence to make the commitment. Then the commitment has to be supported by the dedication to follow through and the execution to apply the measures necessary to get the results you want to achieve."

Then he added a pair of Fs that he believes are attributes of successful small business owners—*focus and flexibility*.

"You start out with goals and objectives, and then you develop a strategy to achieve those goals and objectives.

"I don't focus on the problem like so many people do, I focus on the solution. You need to understand the problem, then understanding the problem you need to develop a solution. But once you do, you need to be totally focused on the solution.

"Then there's flexibility. In the banking business, guys like me were brought up to be inflexible; we were bound by rules and regulations and procedures and a lot of our performance measures were based on our adhering to those policies and procedures.

But as the banking industry has changed, we learned you have to be more flexible because things are happening faster and with greater magnitude."

Others we have talked with, men and women who are models of business success, all have their own ABCs to share. Here are some:

A is for ABILITY.
F is for FAMILY.

David Lizarraga says, "Having vision or desire to do something is important, but if you don't have the *ability* to implement it, it's just a dream. What you need to do is keep working ahead, keep pressing at the envelope, always challenging yourself to do more. You learn that whatever asset you have is a precious asset. There is no substitute for hard work."

"You have to have your *family* aligned with what it is you are trying to accomplish in business. So many new businesses that start out are to some degree or another family-owned businesses, and if the family is not united in what is trying to be accomplished the business is almost surely doomed to failure. Then too, having balance is important too. By this he means that while you're spending the time necessary to start and build your business you still must allow time for those other facets of your life that are important—particularly family."

D is for DETERMINATION.
G is for GOALS and for GLOBAL.

Harold E. Doley says, "I think I'm a success because I'm *determined*. I've been determined all my life. You have to be able to look at the situation, analyze it, and make a decision. You don't have the luxury of being able to ponder and ponder and ponder. Every day I have to make snap decisions. You have to recognize when you're right, and when you wrong, and if you're wrong how to correct your course.

"Every year I begin the year with my *goals* for the coming year, what I want to accomplish that year, and what I want to accomplish in the years ahead. It is a short-term plan and the long-term plan. I think it's critical to define your goals then to deal with the steps that are required to achieve those goals."

"Today, you have to think *globally*. With today's economic system, with the communications system, you have to look broadly and globally in terms of your horizons. After you get your base, you need to look beyond the rainbow. It's a global investment world, it's a global market. That's the future."

A is for ATTITUDE.
V is for VALUES.
S is for SMART.
G is for GOALS.

Fred Ruiz says, "Running a business is an up-and-down roller coaster ride forever. I think the most important thing is that you keep a positive *attitude*. You can't get down, period. I've learned that if you just keep at it you can get by any problem. You just can't quit. And you have to trust your people because they're always part of the solution. I guess I'm not one of those lucky people who can be a success without working very hard. For me, success takes a lot of hard work.

"When I talk to young people, the first thing I tell them is there's a great deal of opportunity out there. But it requires hard work to be successful. Work hard, have a positive attitude.

"*Values* are very important when you run a business, and for your customers your employees your venders. Honesty and fairness are keys. Whoever you're doing business with, it's a partnership. If it is a partnership, then both people win. If I win, and my vendors lose, then it's not a very good partnership and not a positive thing because in the long run those vendors are going to be gone. But when I win, and they win also, we're going to be able to take it to another level and grow together.

"I get very upset when I see people who are successful begin to throw it all away because they get greedy. They begin to cheat their employees, or treat their customers poorly, or cheat the government and end up just throwing all away."

We saw the following in Chapter 8, but it's worth repeating here.

"In business, you do have low points where it's difficult to see the light at the end of the tunnel. I can remember when we first started our business, the first five years was hand to mouth. We got to the point where I sat down and doing the books I saw all the money that we owed to our vendors and looked at the amount of money that was coming in, and I said it looks like we have about two weeks left and then we're going to have to close the doors. My dad's response was, 'well, I guess we'll have to work a little harder.'

"What he actually meant was not that we have to work a little harder, but rather we have to work a little *smarter*. So we looked around at the marketplace and we came up with a new product—tamales—and we took the product to a lot of smaller retailers, mom-and-pop kinds of operations, and the timing was just perfect. It turned out to be an instant success. This got us over the hump, and we were able to weather our financial difficulties. We learned a lot from this experience—about how to market new products and about how to take advantage of some of the changing facets of society such as women working outside the house and needing ways to quickly and easily fix dinner when they got home.

"The bottom line is we were able not to work harder, but to work smarter, and that was a really important lesson to learn. It was an important lesson because truthfully, I thought we were done.

"When I started at 21 years old, I thought that if I retired at age 65 and Ruiz Foods was a $3-million-year business, I would've been a tremendous success. And here we are a half billion dollar a year company, and on our way to becoming a billion-dollar company, and I'm not done yet. I think setting goals is really important, but you have to keep adjusting those *goals*."

Susan Au Allen is the president and CEO of the U.S. Pan Asian American Chamber of Commerce. Since 1984, USPAACC has promoted economic growth for Asian American businesses and professionals. There are over 1.2 million Asian American firms in the United States, which represents 27 percent of all minority-owned businesses in this country. Asian American-owned businesses accounted for a gross receipt of $306 billion or

51.3 percent of the $598.2 billion revenue of all minority-owned businesses in the most recent year that numbers are available. Asian American-owned businesses employed more than 2.2 million workers.

Susan herself is a successful entrepreneur and a long time observer of small business and what small business owners do right and what they do wrong. She believes:

H is for HARD WORK.
C is for the CUSTOMER.
P is for PERSONAL TOUCH.

"Nothing replaces *hard work,* which is first and foremost. Nothing replaces a willingness to work hard, to work long hours especially at the beginning. You must be consistent; you must have repetition. You must do it over and over again so you can become perfect at what you do. You must specialize; you must be a specialist in something instead of a generallist in nothing.

"In your business, your *customer* is king. It takes a long time to develop a customer but it only take one day, one incident, to lose that customer; so always be looking at what more you can do for your customer.

"Many small business owners are shortsighted. They say 'I'm too busy I can't get out and I can't leave the office or the factory because I need to be here to do the work. But when you're an entrepreneur your role is to build the business, to grow it, because you are the business, you are the face of the business. Your customer wants to see you. Too many small business owners would like to stay hunkered down in the shop, and will never go out to see the customers.

"Today, when so much business is conducted online, there is no more *personal touch.* That personal touch is very important. It can make or break your business. Even if your business operates on a small margin, that low margin can be enhanced by going out to the person you want to talk to, or sell to.

"The mistake small business owners make is they do not go out often enough and see the real world and as a result they miss opportunities. You have to be out there on the front line hearing and seeing what the customer needs, and what the customer is saying about you and your product. Then you also know what your competitors are doing, which is critical."

S is for SERVICE.
H is for HONESTY.
N is for NEVER QUIT.
C is for CARING.

Thanh Quoc Lam says, "I never felt that I wouldn't make it and I never felt like quitting. There are many times when I got very tired. When I did, I thought back to what I had when I first came to America, and what I have now, and it gives me the incentive to push forward.

"*Service* and *honesty* are important if you're going to do business. You must have respect for your employees, and for your customers, and for your product. You should not do things to your employees, or to your customers, that you would not want people to do to you. I see a situation where someone is in business and they treat the same customer differently when they first do business with them than they do two years later when they have established a relationship. That's wrong. You should treat the customer as if he's an old customer the very first day you do business with him. Also the opposite they treat the customer very well when they're first starting out, but then later when they're making money and they don't need to depend on that customer, they treat them poorly.

"People don't care what you know until they know you *care.*"

F is for FOCUS
R is for REPUTATION.

Bob Wright adds, "In starting out, you have to stay *focused*. You have to work through the difficult times. I often see people starting out in business who are simply not very patient. You have to have patience. You have to have a game plan and you have to stick with it.

"The main lesson I think I've learned over the years is that in business it is a lot about relationships. It's a lot about how people view you—not only your customers but people who work for and with you. There has to be a mutual level of respect. This is especially true in performing work within the government. It's almost like credit, if you have good credit you can go a long way but if you have bad credit no one's going to give you very much. In doing business with the government it's all about past performance and *reputation*. What you've done in the past weighs heavily on how well you will do in the future. If you've been satisfying your customers, living up to your commitments and making the customers look good, if you have been operating with honesty and integrity and doing things the right way, then you can be very successful."

D is for DIRECTION.
S is for SENSE OF HUMOR.

Linda Alvarado says, "You have to have a sense of *direction* and have goals. More than that, you have to have a sense of how you're going to get there. I call it a blueprint. There is no perfect blueprint. It always changes. There has to be a sense of commitment as to what you're going to do. The how can change while you're trying to achieve a sense of balance. It not just about volumes and profits and stature, you need a sense of balance with your family and your community.

"An important attribute is a sense of *humor* because not everything is going to go well. We need to learn not to make fun of others, but we need to know we can still have fun on even the most challenging of days."

P is for PASSION.

LuLu Sobrino contributed, "You have to have the *passion*. Yes, you have to find your niche, but if you don't love your business, if you don't use all your energy there's noting you can do because you are going to have all kinds of obstacles. Without the passion you're not going to make it because the first thing bad that happens you're going to give up."

T is for TOUGHNESS.
P is for PERSISTANCE and PEOPLE.

Bob Lotter added, "To be successful, I think, you have to be a bit *tough,* you have to be stubborn. You can't be willing to give up. I think the bottom line for me is I came from a lower middle class family, I went into the army so I would have money for college, I went to college while I was in the army so nothing I did in my life came easy. Nobody gave me anything. Nobody loaned me money. No one ever bought me a car. So my whole life has been a series of small challenges. But that's just part of life and you have to be willing to face up to those kinds of things.

"There are a lot of great ideas out there, we've all heard them. But it seems that some of the greatest ideas never come to fruition. So what is the difference between having a great idea and having one and bringing it to fruition? The difference between being an entrepreneur and being a want-to-be is *persistence* because there is usually no easy way. About 99 percent of the time it's difficult and it takes a lot of hard work. You're going to make mistakes. It's not going to work out the way you hoped. You're going to have to have the intestinal fortitude and integrity and the willingness to remake yourself over and over again—whatever it takes to succeed while at the same time maintaining a balance so it doesn't just become the pursuit of money, since you don't want to lose touch with other parts of life while you're on that journey.

"The money will come, but you have to do the right thing. It's not selfless to treat other *people* right. In the long run it's self-preservation.

"Don't do anything just for money. If you're goal driven and most entrepreneur are and you want to be wealthy and have that big house on the hill don't forget you're not going to get there by yourself. It's a much more fun game if you bring people along for the ride and you get more out of it. I don't remember the biggest check I have ever gotten. I can't tell you how much it was or when I got it. But I can remember being embraced by a 67-year-old guy at an awards ceremony with tears streaming down his face saying 'You changed my life.' Those are the moments I remember the most."

V is for VISION.
P is for PASSION.

Melanie Sabelhaus says, "My advice to women entrepreneurs, and really to all entrepreneurs, is the first thing you have to be able to do in your heart and in your mind, is paint that *vision* of what this business is all about, and what you believe it can achieve; and this is whether you are starting the business, or trying to grow it. This vision has to be so crystal clear that everybody understands it and falls in love with it—your customers and your employees. You must review that vision on a constant basis.

"Then you must have *passion*. If you don't have passion, don't even bother getting your own business. Passion is contagious and everyone around you will feel it."

P is for PATIENCE and PURPOSE (and PERSISTENCE).
F is for FOCUS.
F is for FEAR.
W is for WILL to WIN.

Mitchell Rubinson tells us, "I mentor a lot of young people who want to get out there in the world into something. There's certain philosophical things I try to instill in them. The most important thing I tell young entrepreneurs is to have patience, persistence, focus, and singleness of purpose. Nothing is going to become successful overnight. It takes tremendous effort and hard work. So you have to be *patient*. You have to be *persistent*. You have to *focus* on that idea and you cannot do multiple things at the same time. You're married to that venture, you really, really have to commit.

"Another thing I think is very important is *fear*. I think fear is the greatest motivator of all. People are afraid to do this or do that. But what they need to do, at least what I do, is to turn that fear into a great motivator. The fear of failure, not wanting to fail, not suffer the embarrassment, is what you need to push yourself further. I think that's very, very important.

"If you ever have a low point all you can do is dig down real deep. You reach way down and say this is not me and I'm not going to allow it to happen. I'm going to make a positive outcome. I'm going to do whatever it takes.

"At one point, I worked 84 hours a week on a business and my attitude was if I worked two weeks for every one I would get there twice as quickly. I've been in highly charged situations that seem to require miracles, or things that were just very, very bleak, that people just don't have the fortitude to escape. To me one of the tests is whether you simply dig down, *focus* on what the issue is, and do whatever it takes to cross the line. The difference between a winner and a loser is the capacity to come back.

"I think I'm a success because I could never afford to fail and I never could give up. I think I'm a success because I can always retain my *focus*.

"The principal character you look for in somebody wanting to start a business is how much they want to *win*. It's how much they want to win. You need to win their willingness to take responsibility for what they are doing. I've learned that if you want something handed to you, don't even start because you're going to fail. To me, the real winners are kids who come from blue-collar families and are very hungry. Their parents may have been electricians, or plumbers, or cleaning people—it doesn't matter, they have the hunger.

"If you have the mindset you really want to win, and you're hungry for success, if you don't think it's ordained to you and you're going to have to put in hard work and you are humble because nobody likes a braggart, there is no question in my mind that one day you'll become a millionaire."

G is for GOALS.
F is for FOCUS.
N is for NEVER GIVE UP.

Rebecca Matthias adds, "I thought a lot about what advice I give to young women wanting to start their own business. I've boiled it down to three things: *Think Big, Focus, and Never Give Up.* I think that anybody who follows those three rules will have a successful business.

Success is a very personal thing. It has to be defined by each person and one person's success cannot necessarily be another person's success. So I think it's important for each person to look into themselves and say 'what we do I want out of life?' You can't answer that question without experimenting a little. You have to try different things. Then you have to look into yourself and find out what's important to you, what's important to your life. Then you can set up *goals,* and when you get there, that's success. It can be very different for different people.

"In my case, the idea of success had different aspects to it. One was combining my family and my business. That was very important to me. I have a lot of goals and a lot of objectives for my business, but I didn't want to do that at the expense of my marriage, my family, my kids. I was able to combine those two things, my business and my family, and make them work together. This was very important to me, and if there's one thing to me that defined success, that was it.

"I like to say 'think big' because that means something to me. But of course, big is different for every person. But think big to me means think bigger—stretch yourself. If you think you can do X, then push yourself to do 2X. That way you might get to X. That gives you a goal, you have to have a horizon, something you're going for. My father always told me to think big. Everyone doesn't have to have the goal of having a public company, a multimillion-dollar company, but even if you only want to have a small company, just think a little bigger and you'll get a little further. You'll only do as much as you try to do and you're not likely to accidentally do more. In fact, it probably will be a little less. So I always try to get people to stretch what they think they can do.

"The *focus* has to do with the fact that there is only 24 hours in the day. So you have to focus on what's really important in your life so if you've made the decision that starting the business is one of those important things you'll probably have to let a few of the things go. You may not be able to do every social event that you did before, or might want to do. But in the long run it's going to be worth it because you're going to achieve what you focus on. So you have to make choices.

"Then you *never give up* because you only fail when you stop trying. There were probably 50 times I thought about just giving my company away, if you'd asked. But somehow, someone forced me to keep going and you find a way. So if you refuse to give up, your company will develop, but perhaps just not in the way you originally thought. In my case, I thought I had a mail-order catalog business, and I don't anymore. My business has changed and transformed so many times. You might change your mind about what it is that you have to stay in the game."

E is for EDUCATION.
C is for CONFIDENCE.

Nina Vaca adds, "I know I needed to learn so much and I'm so glad I've been able to surround myself with people I can learn from. When your business is small you have to learn. When my business was small I had to learn about benefits, and health care, and payroll and finance and all these other things. I just wanted to run my business, but there were all these things I just had to know and I had become an expert in all these other things. As your business grows there's so much you always have to learn. I'm a staunch advocate of *education*, not just through college, but even later even if you're an entrepreneur. For instance I've been to every executive management program I can find that will benefit me. And I still don't know it all; I accept the fact that I don't.

"You can't do anything in the world of business without *confidence*. As an entrepreneur you do need someone to have faith in you, to believe in you. It can be your partner, your banker, your wife or husband, or whoever it is. Entrepreneurship means a lot of rejections, so if you don't have confidence starting out, you will have problems."

T is for TENACITY.
P is for PERSEVERENCE.

Al Frink adds to the ABCs with, "I believe I'm a success because I've always believed that failure is simply unthinkable. I simply cannot accept failure. I have always believed that failure is not an option. Desire and the willingness to pay the price are what is needed. It's a question of *tenacity* combined with your God–given skill that pushes you ahead so you shouldn't fail.

"I really had two challenges. The first was a personal challenge: did I have the confidence to reach a certain level of success? The second challenge was trying to build a business from scratch. The two challenges were actually very similar in that both require you to prove yourself. In both cases, you need *perseverance,* which I consider a major attribute of success.

"You talk to the person who runs a business, and almost always they'll tell you there are times when they wonder if they can make their payroll. You think of all these difficulties, but you don't give up. You realize you owe it to yourself, you owe it to the people around you, and you owe it to your pride not to let fear stop you from pressing forward, especially if you believe in what you're doing."

P is for PRIORITIZE.

Let me add one here. You should *prioritize* your work. The As, the Bs and the Cs. Always do the As first, even if you can't finish them. These are critical and can't wait. Then the Bs medium in importance. Often Cs can wait, and many drop off the list before you even notice it. It's important not to do just what you like. Remember, successful people do what failures won't.

14

You Can and Will Succeed

The purpose of this book has been to assist entrepreneurs and enroll them in an incredibly rewarding life as a small business owner. Webster's definition for entrepreneur is: "Someone who organizes a business venture and assumes the risk for it." It's from the French word *entreprendre* meaning to undertake.

It is a simple definition, but one that shows the prominence of risk in the entrepreneurial equation. But at the same time, from my experience, it may not be entirely correct.

I have known and worked with many in government who are entrepreneurial. Likewise, I have met large numbers of workers in big business—in publicly traded companies—who are entrepreneurial in their outlooks and treat their jobs with that spirit. Many of the best people I have worked with from nonprofit organizations are committed entrepreneurs. Alternatively, I have known more than one business owner—some very successful—who clearly are not entrepreneurial, although I have to wonder how they have managed to get where they are.

I have attempted to show by examples of many people who have had success in business what it takes to be successful. They have discussed the key issues and problems associated with those issues, and commonsense solutions for overcoming those problems in order to be successful.

We've learned how important it is not to make it up on the fly. I have often said I would rather learn from the mistakes of others than repeat those mistakes myself. It doesn't mean you can't or shouldn't or won't make a mistake. It just means, to the extent that you can minimize those mistakes, you can be much more effective in accomplishing your goals.

It's clear how important it is not to assume anything. You have to start with the premise that there is much to learn. There is much you don't know. The good news is we have provided a significant number of resources for you to use.

You have to dare to be different and just because someone tells you it's never been done before doesn't mean you have to accept that. At the same time, you should research others who have attempted a similar business. There may be a reason why your brilliant idea will not work.

Accept the fact that anything significant is going to take a certain amount of risk on your part. I have learned that the critical aspect is to take a *calculated* risk, a *measured* risk, and not risk the farm.

You also have to find your advantage. I've heard it described as your distinct competitive advantage. This will be important as a way of distinguishing and separating yourself from the pack, especially if you are in an industry with many similar competitors.

I have often said that I can't accomplish anything important by myself. I know that to be true, and many of our success stories emphasize it and acknowledge the critical importance of other people. You will rise or fall depending on who is on your team. This may be one of the most important keys to success.

It's also important not to assume anything. Remember, it's not a question of *if,* but *when,* something will threaten your business. It may be a natural or a man-made disaster. The key is to survive it, to get to the other side, and be better and stronger in spite of it.

After the principles, we provided tangible tools for success. If you surround businesspeople with all of the tools they need to succeed, they can do the rest.

It's important for a budding entrepreneur to know where to go to get help and critical answers. I have frequently heard a businessperson say, "I wish I would have known where to get that help or learn about that program. It would have made my life a lot easier."

So, that is one of the most important benefits of this book—now you know. There are more volunteers and inexpensive providers of counseling and technical assistance than ever before. In addition, you could spend months going online to web sites that are dedicated to helping a new entrepreneur. This will only increase in the future.

It's important not to fall into the "analysis paralysis" trap. We have tried to give you the best of the best in terms of options. This by no means is the only list of resources available and you should always keep abreast of the changes in your industry and the new information to remain at the forefront of your business and industry.

One of the tools that will never change for the rest of your life in business is the importance of technology. This truly is what levels the playing field, which allows the smallest businesses to be competitive with much larger companies.

I heard someone say that we should think of technology like we think of electricity. In other words, we take electricity for granted. It is ubiquitous. When you turn on the light switch, the lights go on.

It wasn't always that way. In fact, business at the turn of the twentieth century was often done by candlelight or lamp. That wasn't that long ago. Now most of us can't explain exactly how electricity and currents work. We just take electricity for granted and depend on it. That is the same relationship we have with technology. But in this case, we need to know how it works and what we need to get the job done. It is not anything we should fear. But we should embrace and apply it whenever possible.

There are some pretty important organizations that want to get to know us and do business with us. They are called the

U.S. government and corporate America. However, we shouldn't assume anything. We need to learn how they work, what they are trying to accomplish, how they win, and if we should pursue them for our mutual benefit. It is also important to break down the barriers that we and others impose on our ability to move forward and succeed. This is critical because we truly have more to offer and more power than we ever admit.

I hope the mystery has been taken out of capital and how to get it. Capital means many things to different people, but at the end of the day it is what sustains a business, whether they are just starting out or are among the largest corporations in the land. Much has changed from the early days and the opportunity to get the financial resources you need has never been better. But just like you have to sell a prospective client, you must also be able to persuade and convince a financial company that you will be a good risk and valuable client to their firm.

A capital infusion in your business is not a right, but that doesn't mean you don't deserve an opportunity to prove yourself. Don't be discouraged, it's not a question of *if* only *when*, if you are willing to do what needs to be done to win. One of my favorite sayings is: "I don't want to be right, I just want to win." Too many people are more concerned with winning the argument. I am content with letting others win the debate, as long as I get in the end zone.

Being right is a matter of opinion, where you stand on an issue, and the judgment you give it. It's not about that for me. It's not about winning the argument regardless of the merit or logic. It's about accomplishing something valuable that will benefit you, and not about "pyrrhic victories."

We heard the ABCs for success from very successful role models. There is no *one way* to be successful. These incredible success stories prove that. There is more than one way to get the job done. It is your responsibility to find the ways that make sense for you. It is important to trust your gut or intuition. That inner voice is often the truth for you. One thing not in dispute is that these individuals are people who have worked a lifetime to build great character and reputation. Everything flows from their commitment to be the best they can possibly be. It's always a work in progress. They are never satisfied that they have truly accomplished their full potential, and that fire in their belly is what keeps them striving to do more. Not for themselves, but for a greater community or vision that they are working for.

There's been much discussion about statistics, and one of my objectives for you was to become part of the success stories and not the failures. It's natural to be cautious or worried about beginning something that you've never done before, but it's critically important not to be afraid to the point you can't generate your success.

One of the things that always motivated me was that I didn't want to ever look back and regret not having done it. I could take not becoming a huge success. I just was not willing to always wonder, "What if?" In fact, one of my favorite quotes is from Thoreau, who said "The mass of men lead lives of quiet desperation." That was unacceptable for me. I never wanted to feel trapped in someone else's business. I always felt that if I was going to work that hard for someone, it should be for myself. Having said that, I have also found small business people who felt trapped in their own business because they weren't winning should never have started that business in the first place.

I have been fortunate to have worked in many different kinds of organizations. I worked for my parents. I worked for other small businesses. I worked for a large corporation. I worked for nonprofits. I even worked for the U.S. government at the highest level, but the most enjoyment, fulfillment, and joy I have ever experienced professionally was being the owner of my own business. It truly has been a great ride, and, God willing, it's not even close to being over.

I believe the opportunities are vast if you learn how to create them for yourself. That attitude comes from within and must be generated. There is no perfect time. You need to visualize what's possible now, in the present, and not wait for someone or something. Someone once told me that if I wanted to be very successful in business, I needed to act and think like a successful person. I didn't really understand what that meant at first. I have also heard it described as being "your future in the present." I now believe that is a very powerful concept that has the potential of unleashing your greatness.

It's also important to have fun and truly enjoy the work and all of the people you share it with. Someone once told me to just concentrate on making money, and later after you make the money, you can do what you really want to do and make yourself happy. Instinctively, I knew I couldn't do that, especially if I was compromising my values and principles in the process.

There are many who are willing to take shortcuts because their business is just a means to an end. Most of the people we have met actually do the reverse. They are occupied in their business as an end in itself. To the extent they do it well provides them with a means for other interests or people in their life. It's important to enjoy the journey because it will be something you do for a long part of your life. It's also important to be in relationships with others. It's not only more fulfilling, but as we have discussed it is essential for building something great. Learn to consistently help others and give back, and you'll be surprised how much of it comes back to you when you least expect it.

Practice character. I truly believe that great character is built one block at a time. Nothing replaces it. If you lose it, it could be difficult, if not impossible, to get it back.

My dad had a saying in Spanish that translated to, "Don't do good things that look bad." He was right.

There is often confusion about what it is that you should choose to be in a business or occupation that will make you happy and provide the rewards to support the kind of life you want to have. However, often people end up in businesses or jobs that they never planned or wanted. Sometimes, it is the trappings of success. Sometimes you get stuck in a job because you believe you can't afford to leave it. Maybe you have gotten used to a certain standard of living and are not willing to give it up even if you are miserable. It could be because of age or dependents or health reasons. My dad would say, "I want to be the architect of my destiny."

General Emiliano Zapata said, "I prefer to die on my feet than live on my knees." That is a bit dramatic, but you get the point.

There has to be an emotional connection for most people who will be successful. If you don't live it and breathe it, it will eventually show up for what it is to those you are trying to enroll in your business.

Harold Doley says, "Every year I begin the year with my goals for the coming year, what I want to accomplish that year, and what I want to accomplish in the years ahead. It is a short-term plan and a long-term plan. I think it's critical to define your goals, then to deal with the steps that are required to achieve those goals."

It's important not to wing it because you can't sell it, if you don't believe in it. If you don't believe in it, why should anybody else? If you're not confident, you should never "write the check." Many small business people sell themselves out of the sale because they are not clear on what the value is that they are offering to a potential client. No one will believe in your business if you really don't.

That is why the clarity and understanding that derives from a good plan is so critical. I asked a wise soul once how to decide this critical question. She said I should imagine I had made $1 billion and I had bought everything I could ever want, I had traveled around the world many times, I had given to all of the charities I cared about, and I had taken care of my family for generations. Now, she asked, what would you be doing to occupy the rest of your life?

It was a great question. It forced me to think about what my passion really was. The point is, if you focus on what you really care about, then it doesn't matter what the financial rewards will be or what others think about your passion because you will be doing something that you were put on this earth to do. It is the kind of work that isn't work. It's the reason you'll jump out of bed in the morning excited and ready to go to your business. It is your higher purpose. And whatever happens, you will be happy and fortunate that you get to do it. Like when someone says, "I would pay them to let me do this, they wouldn't have to pay me." Interestingly, this is when you're truly in a position of power and will produce the results and rewards you've always dreamed of. I believe this is where true opportunity and success lives.

Finally, you have to understand what you can control, and what you never will. Many things happen in our life, and we have a great power to deal with them. We get to determine what we will do with those things and how we will think about them and react to them. We take control. We don't have to give it up to someone or something. You've heard this before, but most of us don't practice it in our daily lives. It is life changing if you assume total responsibility for your life no matter what happens.

Across from my desk in my office is a poster listing H. Jackson Brown Jr.'s "21 Suggestions for Success." He is the insightful author of books like *Life's Little Instruction Book* (Nashville, TN: Thomas Nelson, 2000). Almost every day I find these suggestions helpful, and I thought you might also:

1. Marry the right person. This one decision will determine 90 percent of your happiness or misery.
2. Work at something you enjoy and that's worthy of your time and talent.
3. Give people more than they expect and do it cheerfully.
4. Become the most positive and enthusiastic person you know.
5. Be forgiving of yourself and others.
6. Be generous.
7. Have a grateful heart.
8. Persistence, persistence, persistence.
9. Discipline yourself to save money on even the most modest salary.
10. Treat everyone you meet like you want to be treated.
11. Commit yourself to constant improvement.
12. Commit yourself to quality.
13. Understand that happiness is not based on possessions, power, or prestige, but on relationships with people you love and respect.
14. Be loyal.
15. Be honest.
16. Be a self-starter.
17. Be decisive even if it means you'll sometimes be wrong.

18. Stop blaming others. Take responsibility for every area of your life.
19. Be bold and courageous. When you look back on your life, you'll regret the things you didn't do more than the ones you did.
20. Take good care of those you love.
21. Don't do anything that wouldn't make your mom proud.

Now, I wish you all the success that this life can provide. I'll be rooting for you from the sidelines.

If you want to contact me about this book, you can do so at *www.theengineofamerica.com*.

What are you waiting for? Get going!

Appendix

Where to Get Help
on the Web

Organizations like SCORE and the Small Business Development Centers should be a first stop for anyone starting a small business or thinking of starting one, or any small business owner whose enterprise is growing, especially those experiencing growing pains.

While it might not substitute for the kind of one-on-one help that a SCORE or SBDC counselor can give, there are many places on the Internet where a small business owner can find a vast array of help and assistance, and possibly can also begin to learn what he or she doesn't know.

Here are 73 web sites that will help you get the information you need.

GOVERNMENT AND GOVERNMENT SUPPORTED

http://www.sba.gov
> The gateway to all the information the U.S. Small Business Administration can provide. Especially valuable is the SBA's almost encyclopedic listing of Internet links of interest to small business owners.

http://www.sba.gov/smallbusinessplanner/start/index.html
> The SBA's guide and tutorial on starting and growing a small business.

http://www.score.org
> SCORE—"Counselors to America's Small Business"—provides entrepreneurs with free, confidential, face-to-face, and online business counseling. Counseling and workshops are offered at 389 chapter offices nationwide by experienced business volunteers. Also useful to locate the SCORE office nearest to you.

http://www.sba.gov/aboutsba/sbaprograms/sbdc/index.html
> Small Business Development Centers home page containing downloadable information. Useful for finding the nearest SBDC.

http://sbdcnet.org
> Small Business Development Center National Information Clearinghouse where you can find a wealth of information that you can view and download.

http://www.pro-net.sba.gov
> PRO-Net—The U.S. Small Business Administration, the Department of Defense, the Office of Management and Budget, and the General Services Administration have taken steps to simplify the federal contracting process by creating an integrated database of small businesses that want to do business with the government. The integration of PRO-Net and DOD's Central Contractor Registration (CCR) databases has created one portal for entering and searching small business sources. This integration assists small businesses with marketing their goods and services to the federal government.

http://www.business.gov

The official business link to the U.S. government is managed by the U.S. Small Business Administration in partnership with 21 other federal agencies. This partnership, known as Business Gateway, is a presidential e-government initiative that provides a single access point to government services and information to help the nation's businesses with their operations.

This site guides you through the maze of government rules and regulations and provides access to services and resources to help you start, grow, and succeed in business. Its "Regional" listing gives in-depth information by state and its "Industries" section gives information and links to in-depth information on a range of different industries.

http://www.aptac-us.org

Where you can find which of the 250 local Procurement Technical Assistance Center offices around the country is nearest you. They provide expertise and counselors to help you sell to the federal government.

http://www.census.gov/epcd/www/naics.html

If you want to do business with a government agency or with many large corporations, you have to know your company's NAICS code(s) that describe the products or services you offer. This site gives you everything you need to know about the system including a helpful resource for looking up specific codes.

http://www.sba.gov/sdb

Direct link to the SBA's Small and Disadvantaged Business program and certification process and documents.

http://www.osdbu.gov

Links to the small business offices of virtually every federal agency.

http://www.fedbizopps.gov

FedBizOpps.gov is the single government point-of-entry (GPE) for federal government procurement opportunities over $25,000. Government buyers are able to publicize their business opportunities by posting information directly to FedBizOpps via the

Internet. Through one portal—FedBizOpps (FBO)—commercial
vendors seeking federal markets for their products and services
can search, monitor, and retrieve opportunities solicited by the
entire federal contracting community.

http://www.firstgov.gov
Entry portal to all government information and web sites.

http://www.gsa.gov
Entry portal to the federal government's procurement arm—the
General Services Administration (GSA).

http://www.gsa.gov/portal/gsa/ep/home.do?tabId=0
Direct link to the GSA's Office of Small Business Utilization.

http://www.cbdnet.gpo.gov
The *Commerce Business Daily* (CBD) lists notices of proposed
government procurement actions, contract awards, sales of government property, and other procurement information. Each edition contains approximately 500 to 1,000 notices.

http://www.whitehouse.gov/omb/egov
Gateway to information about the federal government's expanding electronic government initiative.

http://www.fedworld.gov
Gateway to government information, managed by the National
Technical Information Service (NTIS) as part of its information
management mandate.

http://www.govloans.gov
Gateway to government loan information. It directs you to the
loan information that best meets your needs. Five federal
agencies—Department of Agriculture, U.S. Department of
Education, U.S. Department of Housing and Urban Development, U.S. Department of Veterans Affairs, and the U.S. Small
Business Administration have come together to create this
single point of access for federal loan information on the Web.

http://www.firstgov.gov/shopping/shopping.shtml
   A complete and constantly updated list of all government sales and auctions.

http://www.fss.gsa.gov
   The GSA's Federal Supply Service (FSS) provides a central source for virtually every commercial product or service a federal buyer might need. It can be used as a definitive reference to meeting the government's needs.

http://www.gsaadvantage.gov
   Where federal purchasers go to shop. Will tell you what the government is buying and from whom.

http://www.fts.gsa.gov
   The GSA's Federal Technology Service (FTS) buys all technology related products and services for the federal government.

http://www.winbmdo.com
   The Small Business Innovative Research (SBIR) and Small Business Technology Transfer (STTR) programs were mandated by Congress to provide research and development support to small businesses (with 500 or fewer employees) to stimulate the conversion of prototype technologies into commercial products.

http://www.irs.gov/businesses/small/index.html
   The Internal Revenue Service's small business and self-employed one-stop resource including tax information and advice for small business owners and the self-employed.

http://www.sbaonline.sba.gov/financing/special/women.html
   The SBA's Women's Business Center.

http://www.womenbiz.gov
   Gateway for women-owned businesses that want to sell to the federal government.

http://www.vetbiz.gov
The Department of Veterans Affairs' Center for Veterans Enterprise, which includes links to Veterans Business Development Officers nationwide and to Veterans Business Outreach Centers nationwide.

http://www.sba.gov/vets
The SBA's Office of Veterans Business Development that is dedicated to serving the veteran entrepreneur by formulating, executing, and promoting policies and programs of the agency that provides assistance to veterans seeking to start and develop small businesses.

http://www1.va.gov/opa/fact/ventfs.html
The VA Center for Veterans Enterprise, a subdivision of the Office of Small and Disadvantaged Business Utilization, was created to make it easier for veterans to establish and expand their businesses. The Center's mission is to promote veterans' business enterprises.

http://www.pueblo.gsa.gov/links/sb1links.htm
Links to government small business publications available from GSA's Federal Citizen Information Center.

http://www.govcon.com/content/homepage/default.asp
Premier sourcing site for public sector contracting.

http://www.ftc.gov/bcp/franchise/netfran.htm
The Federal Trade Commission's site on franchising.

http://www.ftc.gov/bcp/conline/pubs/invest/buyfran.htm
The Federal Trade Commission's "Consumer Guide to Buying a Franchise."

http://www.uspto.gov
The U.S. Patent and Trademark Office's (USPTO) main web site giving a vast array on patent and trademark information, including how to apply.

http://12.46.245.173/cfda/cfda.html
The *Catalog of Federal Domestic Assistance* includes all 1,424 federal programs, projects, services, and activities that provide assistance or benefits to the American public.

PRIVATE SECTOR

http://www.dnb.com/us
   Dun & Bradstreet—the site to obtain a "DUNS Number" the starting point in doing business with the federal government.

http://smallbusiness.dnb.com/default.asp?bhcd2= 1076940276
   Dun & Bradstreet Small Business Solutions—Get the critical insight and tools you need to grow and protect your business.

http://www.veteranscorp.org
   The Veterans Corporation, a government-funded private entity that provides a source for current and prospective veteran business owners, and for companies interested in working with veteran-owned businesses.

http://www.boots2business.com
   Boots2Business, a program of the Veterans Corporation, presents the leading online resources in education and workplace training, uniquely tailored to meet the needs of America's military personnel, including Guard and Reserve, Veterans, Service-Disabled Veterans, and their families.

http://www.elitedvbe.org/dvbemambo/index.php
   The Disabled Veterans Business Enterprise (DVBE) Network is an organization comprised of certified Disabled Veteran's Business Enterprises. The purpose of the DVBE Network is to provide a forum where members meet to discuss the benefits of membership.

http://www.onlinewbc.org
   An array of resources for women-owned businesses and for women considering starting a small business.

http://www.eventuring.org/eship/appmanager/eventuring/ eventuringdesktop
   The Ewing Marion Kauffman Foundation's Kauffman eVenturing™ site provides a guide for entrepreneurs on the path to high growth. The site provides original articles written by entrepreneurs for entrepreneurs and aggregates "the best of the best"

content on the Web related to starting and running high-impact companies.

http://www.uschamber.com/sb
The U.S. Chamber of Commerce's Small Business Center.

http://www.nfib.com
The National Federation of Independent Business is a small business advocacy association, with offices in Washington, DC, and all 50 state capitals.

http://www.thelatinocoalition.com
The Latino Coalition is an organization that benefits all Hispanic businesses.

http://www.ushcc.com
The U.S. Hispanic Chamber of Commerce (USHCC) provides a number of services to Hispanic-owned small business.

http://nhbic.org
The National Business Information Clearinghouse and Entrepreneurial Development Center provides a bilingual web site with free information on capital formation, access to markets, and management training.

http://www.nationalbcc.org
The National Black Chamber of Commerce with its many state and local chapters is dedicated to helping the African American small business owner.

http://www.nfwbo.org
The National Federation of Women Business Owners' Center for Women's Business Research provides in-depth information about women-owned business.

http://www.uspaacc.com/uspac
The U.S. Pan Asian American Chamber of Commerce (USPAACC) provides in-depth help and networking for Asian American business owners.

http://www.fraud.org
The National Consumers League's fraud information web site.

http://www.allbusiness.com
Helps entrepreneurs, small and growing businesses, consultants, and business professionals save time and money by addressing real-world business questions and presenting practical solutions. The site offers resources including how-to articles, business forms, contracts and agreements, expert advice, blogs, business news, business directory listings, product comparisons, business guides, a small business association, and more.

http://www.work.com
The entrepreneur's manual on where to go, what to know, and how to get the most value from the ever-growing array of Web resources for the small business owner/operator. It is comprised of more than 1,000 how-to guides written by business experts.

http://www.myownbusiness.org
A nonprofit organization whose web site provides free information on starting a business including basic dos and don'ts. It also has available a low-cost 14-session course designed to help owners of small and medium-size businesses identify, understand, and overcome the challenges they will face on a daily basis.

http://www.toolkit.cch.com/tools/tools.asp
Commerce Clearing House's (CCH) Business Owners Toolkit including the CCH Small Business Guide offering a wide range of advice on small business issues including "business, tax, and legal questions and to get practical tips that will help you work smarter, save money, and stay in compliance with the law."

http://www.hp.com/sbso/index.html
Hewlett-Packard's small business site offering free downloadable business templates and a free online learning center.

http://smallbusiness.yahoo.com
Yahoo's small business site offering free advice and links to providers of small business services.

http://www.businessknowhow.com

Award-winning small business web site for home offices and small businesses. Owned by Attard Communications, Inc., Business Know-How is known for providing practical information tools and resources for starting, growing, and managing small and home-based businesses.

www.bplans.com

Owned and operated by Palo Alto Software, Inc. as a free resource to help entrepreneurs plan better businesses. Contains the largest single collection of free sample business plans online. In addition, it has helpful tools and know-how for managing your business, including practical advice on planning, interactive tools, and a panel of experts who have answered more than 1,400 questions from people like you.

www.itssimple.biz/biz_tools

Thousands of pages of information and tools to help you start, run, and grow a successful small business. You'll find ready-to-use business tools including model business documents, financial spreadsheet templates, checklists, and official government forms.

www.morebusiness.com

The Business Resource Center, developed by entrepreneurs for entrepreneurs, provides a wealth of useful articles, business tips, insight, a free Intranet, and other material to help small businesses grow—all free.

www.officedepot.com/renderStaticPage.do?context=/content &file=/businesstools/sbh/default.jsp

Office Depot's very helpful *Small Business Handbook* tells you everything you need to know to run your business, from equity to employees.

www.smallbizu.org/idoc

Online university that teaches the 3Ms: Money, Marketing, and Management.

http://www.inc.com

INC Magazine's online resource center for small business.

http://www.microsoft.com/smallbusiness/hub.mspx
Microsoft's small business resource center contains numerous articles and advice on small business solutions.

http://www.myownbusiness.org
My Own Business, Inc., a not-for-profit public service organization, offers a range of free online courses teaching people how to run their own businesses.

http://www.startupjournal.com
The *Wall Street Journal*'s Startup Journal gives current, useful information about business opportunities, franchising, financing, e-commerce, and running a business.

http://www.eonetwork.org
The Entrepreneurs' Organization (EO) is a global community of 6,500 plus business owners, all of whom run companies that exceed $1 million in revenue. Its mission is to build the world's most influential community of entrepreneurs and it offers forums and help for owners of growing businesses to help them reach that million dollar goal.

http://www-304.ibm.com/jct03004c/businesscenter/small business/us/en?
IBM's small business resource center includes solutions, resources, and financing information. It also allows you to e-mail questions in on your small business problems.

http://www.startupnation.com/index.asp
Gives a wide range of advice and resources for starting or growing a business.

http://www.cnet.com/4520–10192_1–6376230-1.html
Technology publisher CNET Networks' small business advice forum.

http://www.aflac.com/us/en/employers/aflacsb.aspx
Aflac, the international insurance giant, provides a wealth of information for the small business owner on a wide range of types of employer provided insurance.

Index